COACHING CHAMPIONS

DEVELOPING YOUNG SPORTSPEOPLE

Tony Gummerson

COACHING CHAMPIONS

DEVELOPING YOUNG SPORTSPEOPLE

A & C BLACK • LONDON

Published in 2005
by A & C Black Publishers Limited
37 Soho Square
London W1D 3QZ
www.acblack.com

ISBN 0 7136 7335 4

A CIP record for this book is available from the British Library.

Note: While every effort has been made to ensure that the content of this book is as technically accurate and as sound as possible, neither the author nor the publisher can accept responsibility for any injury or loss sustained as a result of the use of this material.

A & C Black uses paper produced with elemental chlorine-free pulp, harvested from managed sustainable forests.

Acknowledgements
Cover photograph © Corbis
Textual photographs by Guy Hearn
Cover design by James Watson

Printed and bound in Great Britain
by Biddles Ltd, King's Lynn

Contents

Acknowledgements

The inspiration for a comprehensive coaching manual such as this came from my long association with a variety of sports in general and very special people in particular.

Wilf Paish, former British Amateur Athletic Federation National Athletics Coach and adviser to Olympic, World, European and Commonwealth champions in a variety of sports, nurtured me as an aspiring athlete to international honours. He was a role model for me and a generation of aspirant teachers of physical education and coaches.

The late, John Horan, 6th Dan Shukokai Karate, former National Coach and adviser to various armed forces in the UK and abroad, World, European and national champions. An inspirational coach and a driving force in developing opportunities for athletes with special abilities.

And all of the sportsmen and women, students and coaches who have had the faith to put their sporting and academic trust in my care. They have, over the past 35 years, enabled me to put theory into practice and tolerated my innovations!

Finally, I want to thank my wife Lin who has endured many lectures on a range of sporting topics particularly when discussing the successes of her beloved Newcastle United.

Introduction

The Changing Nature of Sport

In recent years enormous amounts of money from industry, business, advertising, promoters, sponsors and the media have been, and continue to be, directed towards sport, recreation and leisure. The sports industry and their advertising have been targeting major international and national events, outstanding performances, personalities, leisure, recreation and lifestyle to satisfy the increasing demand for product promotion and entertainment. The worlds of sport, recreation and leisure are an accepted part of the entertainment industry and have to feed an ever-increasing demand for top performances and performers. The traditional professional sports can no longer meet the demand, and, increasingly, sporting entrepreneurs are turning towards amateur sports to meet it. These new sports are having to adopt a more professional attitude in terms of marketing and performance. The industry and the public at large constantly seek higher standards.

Governments are also keen to develop elite performances on the world stage, which serve as an opportunity to promote the country politically, ideologically, economically from related investment, commercially from tourism, culturally, and in an ambassadorial role on the international scene. Associated benefits of promoting participation in some form of physical activity are seen to be advantageous in producing a healthier population while at the same time reducing expenditure on healthcare provision.

The present crop of sporting talent which pervades all aspects of the media and international competitions owes its existence to traditional attitudes towards sport, performance development and career opportunities. With extremely large amounts of money available from industry, business and government sources, sports are rapidly restructuring and reinventing themselves to meet the changing situation; the new Olympic sport of beach volleyball is an excellent example. Governing bodies of sport are radically modifying their coaching strategies, talent identification and performance development programmes to meet the demands being placed on them. The influx of money has created a new concept in employment and vocational opportunities in sport that transcends the old professional and amateur divide. The introduction and development of agents for players and managers in soccer is part of this phenomenon.

All sports have vested interests in identifying and developing young talent. New stars facilitate national and international success and increase the sport's image. Sir Steve Redgrave has been credited with single-handedly raising the profile of rowing as a sport in the UK, and the associated haul of medals at the Athens Olympics. This increased status encourages more participants to take up the activity and generates additional funding. Parents see the personal and financial opportunities for their children, and themselves, available through sporting openings and potential careers. Government, through the revision of the National Curriculum, has seen fit to identify a strategy for physical development and also a mechanism for performance enhancement. With central government funding, partnerships with sports governing bodies and local authorities, centres of excellence, sports academies, are being built. Further, there is increasing provision for the development of sporting facilities in schools and colleges generally, and a raft of other strategies increase participation levels and standards of performance.

There has been much discussion and research on the various difficulties that coaching young athletes presents, as with the *wunderkinders* of sport, such as Tiger Woods and Wayne Rooney. However, all parties admit that for the development of any sport catching them young and nurturing their talent is vital. The paradox is to develop sporting talent without creating the physical and psychological problems that have occurred in the past. *Coaching Champions* identifies current best practice in coaching young athletes and its practical application.

In the UK there are over 3,000 primary and 4,000 secondary schools, millions of potential champions! With such a wealth of talent a more structured approach needs to be developed to increasing the grassroots level of participation while at the same time creating a more systematic process to enable everyone to achieve their potential. Apart from the pleasure and health-related benefits of physical exercise there are over 180 governing bodies of sport all offering competitive, financial and career opportunities to the aspiring champion.

Developing a Strategy for Sport

Sport has become such a central feature of popular culture that it has been identified as a vehicle for social change. Taking part and spectating can be seen as an opportunity to develop personal skills and an appreciation of what is required to produce quality in physical activity. It can also create an understanding of the related benefits of physical and mental wellbeing and used as a strategy for modifying anti-social behaviour. The range of activities and the possibilities for participants are greater now than they have ever been. It is this potential wealth of riches that attracts participants, families and coaches. However, the very range of opportunities on offer can obscure the difficulties that can arise, especially with young performers.

The problem with sport, as with many other aspects of society, is that everyone involved has his or her own opinion on how it should be organized and run. With the development of sporting talent, parents, teachers, coaches, sports governing bodies, national agencies and even the government each have their own particular perspective. Whereas there is an ever-growing body of related research which enables a more scientific approach to the identification, nurturing and development of talent, more often than not other factors seem to prevail.

'Maximum athletic performance cannot be explained by physiology alone,' says Dr Roger Bannister. As the world's first sub-four-minute miler and a highly respected medical practitioner, his perspective requires some degree of consideration!

In attempting to analyse the various elements required in coaching champions and explain their scientific underpinning a little knowledge can be a dangerous thing: 'Paralysis by analysis'?

More than a superficial idea of the theories of eminent acknowledged experts and research and their practical application is needed. The situation is further complicated when, like all authorities on any subject, they inevitably disagree. The essentials of best practice will be set out, from a theoretical and applied perspective. It will serve as a platform for athletes, parents, coaches, teachers, students and all others interested for their own particular knowledge, understanding and personal development.

Research, evidence, best practice and opinions comprise the database of the current efforts of all involved. Often they are associated to a greater or lesser degree with myths, anecdotal evidence, established practice, gut instinct and wishful thinking. The difficulty lies in the fact that by and large those involved in the promotion and development of talent mean well, and that their interpretation of related factors are as vital a part of the process as their own professional or personal commitment. With a more enlightened strategical approach many now recoil from past practices which were at best ineffective and at worst counter-productive and injurious. There is now a genuine desire to move the process forward in a mutually advantageous manner for the benefit of the individual athletes and their sports.

There are distinct areas that will influence the participation of young talent, nurture and develop it. Though these will be examined in more detail in later chapters it is important that they are considered from the outset. It is self-evident that in identifying and developing talent there is a chronological time-frame. Those with an interest in teenage and adolescent athletes might wonder why there is an emphasis on the infancy and childhood period. Those with an interest in mature athletes might similarly feel that anything other than the age range that they are dealing with is irrelevant. The fact of the matter is that for the process to be successful there needs to be a clear understanding of the whole picture to enable an appreciation of how the stages fit together into an integrated and mutually dependent structure.

As with any area of particular interest and discussion, expert opinions will on the one hand vary and on the other be totally contradictory! However, in a sporting context, there does *seem* to be a consensus that development of talent falls into four age ranges, which seem to mirror maturational changes, to a greater or lesser degree. These are:

- birth to 8 years
- 8–16 years
- 16–25 years
- 25 years and over.

Immediately there are those who claim that this is not the case and give anecdotal evidence of specific individuals. There are always going to be those athletes who display precocious talent, but these are the exception rather than the rule. For the vast majority the stages identified will serve.

It can be seen that there are going to be major influences that will impact on individuals during these periods. Briefly these include:

Family and Friends

There is the accepted theory that physical and mental attributes required for success in any activity are inherited from one's parents: 'A good athlete is born not made.' It is said that without the physical and mental potential for excellence the development of any ability is hampered, and that no amount of training and coaching can make up for the lack of innate potential. It is suggested by many that, 'You can't put in what the good Lord left out!' and that, 'The careful selection of one's parents is the first step any athlete must take on the road to success!'

Even if this theory is correct, and there are contrary views that will be discussed later, a child blessed with potential must still have an environment that is conducive to the development of positive attitudes to physical activity, along with other socially acceptable qualities. Parents and immediate family are the front line in providing suitable opportunities and inculcating the physical and intellectual qualities required. Difficulties can arise with caring and enthusiastic parents who might wish to relive their sporting dreams and aspirations through their children, or lack the knowledge or information to make considered judgements that might have long-term consequences for their children. Providing the information for parents and family to have positive input and give accurate guidance is currently not an item high on many sports' agendas – a situation that needs speedy revision.

As the athlete matures and develops social interests and friends, these peer-group pressures will affect how he or she participates and performs. With the added responsibilities of personal relationships and financial necessities, additional factors emerge.

The School

Youngsters spend a large part of their formative years in nurseries and schools. Here they learn the essential knowledge and skills to prepare them for life. The importance that the school later places on academic, social and sporting success will have a marked influence on the attitudes the pupils develop to those elements. Positive attitudes to the value, opportunity, nurturing, identification and development of talent start early! It is self-evident that those with the skills of pedagogy both academically and physically are better placed to monitor and develop the intellectual and physical changes associated with infancy, childhood and adolescence.

The school curriculum has to take into account maturational changes associated with age. The physical education programme has to develop crude patterns of movement and refine them into identifiable skills that will form the basis for all the team sports and individual activities later on. Most countries have a national structure for the teaching of physical skills. In the UK the National Curriculum for Physical Education identifies four key stages of development. These include:

Key Stage 1: Ages 4–7

- with guidance perform a range of single skills and linked coordinated movements
- improve their competence through practice.

Key Stage 2: Ages 7–11

- work intensely for a sustained period
- with guidance perform complex skills and coordinated sequences of movements
- begin to select appropriate action to given sporting situations.

Key Stage 3: Ages 11–14

- under guidance improve technical and tactical competence in a wide range of activities
- improve specific skills and complex coordinated sequences of movements
- begin to develop specific elements of fitness.

Key Stage 4: Ages 14–16

- continue to refine and develop technical and tactical competences in a wide range of activities
- specialise in a single or very limited number of activities
- develop sport-specific fitness.

Opportunities have to be provided for the development of specific physical and sporting skills in the lesson and additionally in extra-curricular sessions. Under the watchful eye of the physical education teacher all youngsters are given the opportunity to experience a breadth of activities and develop, in a safe and enjoyable environment, specific skills appropriate to their age, ability and inclination.

The Coach and the Sport

Whereas the school curriculum provides a wide range of sporting opportunities, the role of the coach is to develop specific skills. Often schools will have links with local clubs and coaches. The role of the coach can be blurred by the fact that some physical education teachers may also be coaches in some sports and bring an additional element of expertise, especially to those pupils who compete for the school. Generally, however, coaches are recognised as those who have sport-specific knowledge, a high level of technical and tactical proficiency and have undergone an extensive period of training with a governing body and obtained recognised coaching qualifications. They often see their role as the first step in the process of providing sport-specific participation opportunities, talent identification and development.

Most sports have developed a progressive age-related structure. In many instances it mirrors more or less the developmental stages identified in the National Curriculum. This parallel system enables coaches to operate alongside and within the educational process. With the encouragement of youngsters to specialise in a particular sport after the age of 16 it is specific links to clubs and coaches that will facilitate elite performance.

Everyone leaves school eventually, and continued participation and improvement in a sport is achieved directly or indirectly through the national governing body. It is therefore vital that the coach is fully aware of the systematic and progressive opportunities that exist within the sport at all levels, quite simply because this is the route to success.

The Integrated Approach

The reality of the situation with regard to opportunity, nurturing, identifying and developing talent is very complex. It is a mix of all elements, each having their own part to play yet each contributing to the whole. Parents, schools, teachers, clubs and coaches have to create an integrated network. Without each one of these essential component parts the process stops. It is their careful coordination that is the key to success. The following chapters will examine these and other related elements and give the reader a broader and deeper perspective of what is a very complicated process.

Throughout the book the terms 'athlete', 'player', 'student', 'youngster', 'child', 'pupil' are used to identify the aspiring champion! The terms are in the main interchangeable and serve to show the range of enthusiastic participants and the terminology of their chosen sporting activity. No sport-specific bias is intended. Similarly coach, teacher, trainer and instructor are used to identify those who would seek to help the aspiring champions on their way. Though there may be subtle pedagogical interpretations they can all be used to describe an individual who seeks to improve the performance of another and should be regarded as such in the context of this book.

CHAPTER 1
A BASIC PHILOSOPHY

The general yardstick for the sporting success of a nation is the number of medals won at an Olympic Games. But, since not all sports are included in the normal range of activities offered, this measure could not be accepted as absolutely accurate. However, since most of the games that have an international competitive structure are included in each Olympics, it does give a reasonable comparison of a nation's sporting prowess. After the 2004 Olympics the issue was raised of talent identification and performance development if we in Great Britain are to achieve the success that the country as a whole seems to demand. Interestingly, table 1.1 shows that Great Britain finished a very creditable tenth.

According to some sources, sport in the UK is in crisis because not enough time is devoted to physical education in schools and there is no national strategy for identifying sporting talent. It is also claimed that there is no strategy for intensive coaching to develop an individual's ability to the very highest level. The argument is given that whereas the UK was once a force to be reckoned with, as with our national games of football and cricket that is no longer the case, and suggests that poor performance is commonplace. It is not wise to generalise but I am sure the picture presented is a familiar one.

Howard Wilkinson, the former Leeds United Manager, was given the responsibility of overhauling the Football Association's strategy for the development of young players. He stated that, 'Coaches abroad rub their hands in glee at the fact we are not making the most of the potential that we have in this country.'

Would this account for our less than successful participation in European and World Cups since 1966? Further, does it explain the large number of overseas players that are signed by FA clubs to bolster the strength of their sides and achieve league and cup success? Is there a similar case for cricket, and other sports?

OLYMPICS 2004 MEDAL TABLE					TABLE 1.1
RANK	COUNTRY	GOLD	SILVER	BRONZE	TOTAL
1	UNITED STATES	35	39	29	103
2	CHINA	32	17	14	63
3	RUSSIA	27	27	38	92
4	AUSTRALIA	17	16	16	49
5	JAPAN	16	9	12	37
6	GERMANY	14	16	18	48
7	FRANCE	11	9	13	33
8	ITALY	10	11	11	32
9	SOUTH KOREA	9	12	9	30
10	GREAT BRITAIN	9	9	12	30
11	CUBA	9	7	11	27
12	UKRAINE	9	5	9	23
13	HUNGARY	8	6	3	17
14	ROMANIA	8	5	6	19
15	GREECE	6	6	4	16
16	NORWAY	5	0	1	6
17	NETHERLANDS	4	9	9	22
18	BRAZIL	4	3	3	10
19	SWEDEN	4	1	2	7
20	SPAIN	3	11	5	19

Ten years ago one of the national agencies involved in performance development and talent identification stated that there had been an increase in the number of youngsters involved in sport. They did, however, suggest that levels of participation tended to be more at the casual or recreational level. Their findings concluded that some youngsters were involved in intensive training and that was due to an increase in sports clubs with higher standards of coaching. The elite sportsmen and women of today owe their success or lack of it to the level of coaching and support they have been given for at least the past ten years! The very same experts who were claiming that everything in the garden was rosy ten years ago are now the very ones who are identifying a problem! Further, if there was an increase in participation at casual and recreational levels ten years ago, why are the same experts claiming that the rise in national obesity is due to a lack of participation in any physical activity? Recent research suggests that the drop-out rate in physical activity on leaving school is over 60 per cent. A confusing picture!

An understanding of some of the key issues in coaching champions and how they are addressed seems essential. It would appear that there are as many philosophies on developing talent as there are interested parties. If we look at how the various organisations create structures for individual progression a clearer perspective of how they contribute to the developmental process might be achieved. If we take a chronological approach to the possibilities on offer it might, hopefully, identify a systematic and progressive programme.

EARLY DAYS

Dr Per-Olof Astrand is an eminent authority on sports physiology and has researched many of the factors which produce sporting excellence. He is quoted as stating, 'To be an Olympic champion, I am convinced that you must choose your parents carefully.'

It would seem that even before birth good luck plays an important part in the future success of an athlete; the embryonic individual is already gifted with the genetic potential of mind and body to succeed in sport. Unfortunately, it would seem that many of us chose our parents with little regard.

Long before the idea of genetic engineering had been developed, this random meeting of parents who had the 'correct credentials' had been addressed. It is alleged that the then East German sports scientists arranged state marriages in an attempt to unite the sporting prowess of two athletes to produce a super athlete. As an example, it is suggested that the marriage of Kornelia Ender and Rolland Matthes, both world-class swimmers, was more than a simple love match.

As important as inherited parental qualities may be, it does leave the vast majority of us at a very early age bemoaning our choice of parents and associated sporting oblivion! But hope is at hand. Not every champion is the offspring of former superstars. Statistically, the majority of future champions come from quite normal backgrounds. Recent research in genetics has identified the fact that talented individuals come from a much broader gene pool than previously thought and that it would appear that determination to succeed and the opportunity to develop potential is far more important. The home environment of a developing champion is vital and serves to reinforce the debate of the importance of nature v. nurture. It would seem that the East Germans were hedging their bets and attempting to get the best of both worlds!

In the early years of a youngster's life, the philosophy of parents and guardians, arguably, is 'To facilitate and encourage the development and future potential of their children.' Infants should be subjected to a wide range of stimuli to aid the development of their senses of sight, sound, touch, taste and smell, and to enable them to improve these qualities by physically interacting with them. Not only will this aid the development of sensory awareness but related integrated movement also. In early childhood language skills begin to develop that enable the youngster to communicate and participate in the whole process. Parents endeavour to provide a wide range of activities and the encouragement that will enable this development to occur, which involves a considerable commitment of their time.

Initially progress is achieved simply through interpersonal contact, but as it develops toys will be introduced to maintain interest. Movement can be encouraged from reaching to grasping; from sitting to crawling and walking; then throwing and catching, running and kicking. Fun, enjoyment and play are the keys to the acquisition of any competences. In an enjoyable situation any individual learns faster and maintains the level of achievement for longer. From the early days of psychology and child development it has been identified that social interaction and play are vital to establish the early learning of infants and to establish a solid foundation of physical, intellectual, behavioural and social skills on which the more advanced characteristics of adolescence and maturity can be built.

Initially, parents, guardians, family and friends are proactive in introducing the child to elementary yet vital skills, but as the child develops so does the inclination and confidence to act independently. Children soon have the need to be active every day, and for ever-increasing periods. Physical activity helps to stimulate all the maturational processes and leads to improved physical and emotional health. Play, and modified sport, offer opportunities for social development as youngsters compare themselves to their friends. Being good at sport is a great asset! Children who are successful in sports are more socially accepted by their peers and seem to have better interpersonal skills. Obviously in sporty families children will be offered the normal opportunities for physical, intellectual and social skills and the extra dimension of specific activities such as handling a bat or racket, or early exposure to swimming.

Recent research seems to add an extra validity to the effect of the home environment on human development. It has been established that in the animal kingdom primates, including humans, go through puberty and the maturational process, by comparison to other species, later in life. This gives young primates the opportunity to stay in the infant stage for longer, playing and learning, developing essential skills. If youngsters matured faster they would have less time to acquire skills and therefore develop fewer aptitudes.

SCHOOL DAYS

There comes a time in every child's life when they have to fly the nest and begin their formal social development in school. For some it is an opportunity for developing interests, knowledge and skills; for others, thankfully the minority, it is filled with dread. Obviously many will have attended pre-school nurseries, kindergartens or play school to begin their journey of enlightenment a little earlier!

In the UK from the age of 5 pupils come under the influence of the National Curriculum. There are specific strategies for individual subjects including physical education. For the young sports star, 'Physical education educates young people in and through the use and knowledge of the body and its movement.'

The Curriculum aims through four Key Stages to promote physical development and the value of engaging in physical activity in school and throughout life, aesthetic appreciation of movement and self-esteem and confidence, which are very worthy principles.

Key Stage 1: Ages 5–7

- Pupils should experience at least five areas of activity, including athletic activities, dance, games, gymnastic activities, adventurous outdoor activities and possibly swimming. The programme should build upon the children's natural enthusiasm for being physically active which has been encouraged by their home environment. The school environment offers more structured and improved opportunities for basic skill development using specialised equipment and guidance.

Key Stage 2: Ages 7–11

- Skills should be refined and children should have the opportunity to experience modified competitive situations. Children should be introduced to modified games and apparatus appropriate to their developmental stage.

Key Stage 3: Ages 11–14

- Skills should be further refined to sport-specific application and children should experience formal sports and games.

Key Stage 4: Ages 14–16

- Youngsters should have the opportunity to develop their levels of skills and develop individual sporting preferences.

The overall philosophy of the National Curriculum has been identified as, 'The entitlement of every school pupil to be given the opportunity to develop skill commensurate with their level of ability and inclination.' This would concur with the ideals of teachers of physical education specifically and educators in general.

Following school, colleges and universities have their own sports clubs and competition structure. Here, there is a patchy provision of coaching which itself can be of varying quality. In schools youngsters face a weekly programme of games and physical education. Those who are enthusiastic or show ability are given additional opportunity to improve their competence in school clubs and teams. There is a structure with which they are familiar and have confidence, which encourages their development. Moving on to further or higher education enables talented individuals to continue to improve, depending on the resources available to them. But, those who seek to go into full-time employment are cast adrift from readily available opportunities.

This break in continuity of provision is now seen as a major difficulty in talent identification, which takes place sometime during school life, and reaches its culmination years later. Put simply, when pupils leave school they drop out of sport. This may be because they are no longer required to take part or cannot be bothered to make the effort to go to a sports centre or club. Identified talent which was nurtured through school is now wasted.

This is not a new phenomenon; as far back as the 1950s the UK identified this post-school drop-out. In the 1960s the Wolfenden Committee identified the break between school and sports governing body opportunities. It identified the problems as being:

- Lack of age-related opportunities. Post-school sports were for adults and were structured and organised accordingly. The cost of joining clubs and organisations was also a major factor.
- Limited contact between schools and local clubs and community groups.
- No integration of school or local clubs to ensure continued participation and progressive development of coaching and performance development.
- Lack of an integrated or coordinated system for talent identification and performance development between all agencies involved.

Despite numerous strategies since including more recently Sport for All, The Youth Sport Trust, Top Sport, Champion Coaching, Active Participation and additional National Lottery funding this haemorrhaging talent continues unabated. The actual drop-out rate seems to vary between 60 and 90 per cent depending on how the definition of participation is used. Though some talent may re-emerge by chance after the post-school gap there is still a major problem, not just in developing elite performers but in the health-related benefits of participation.

SPORTS GOVERNING BODIES

The national governing bodies of all sports have the responsibility of organising a structure to offer a comprehensive programme of competitions, coaching, talent identification and performance development to engage participants of all ages and abilities. They do this through a system that includes national, regional, county and local organisations, the classic point of contact being the local club. Most governing bodies have a link directly in the school setting with national associations, such as the English Schools Athletic Association, which organise local, regional, national competitions and championships. Many teachers, especially physical educationalists, have personal and professional involvement in specific sports and naturally create a sequential progression from school to club.

However, these links, if they exist, are tenuous, since they depend upon the tradition of the school, whether it is soccer or rugby focused, for instance, the interests of the PE staff and the local sporting opportunities. There is as yet no formal structure that integrates these various agencies into a progressive and coordinated system, though such strategies are now being considered.

National governing bodies (NGBs) train officials to administer, organise and officiate in a comprehensive national and international competition structure for adults and specific age groups. In order to facilitate this *raison d'être* a comprehensive education and monitoring programme exists, especially in coaching, where there is an equally comprehensive national structure. While an athlete is at school she or he can enjoy the luxury of competing in school and NGB organised competitions. Though colleges and universities have their own sports associations, at some stage the only avenue open to an athlete for competition or development is that of the NGB.

It has been suggested that the internal and external structures that exist with NGBs give rise to a philosophy of, 'The creation of links that will assist towards a talent identification programme'. Though NGBs run leagues and competitions for players of all abilities who desire to achieve success in major international events, there is an underlying search to identify talented individuals and maximise their performance at all levels.

The development of an individual's abilities within the sporting context is in the main down to the influence of the coaches he or she works with. Coaches tend to migrate to levels of coaching that suit their ability and aspirations. Some specialise with young novices, others with adults. Some work with elite individuals or teams, others develop sports participation. Some work within a highly competitive structure, others in a more leisurely and less stressed environment.

Every coach will have her or his own philosophy, but perhaps a common theme would be 'To enable an athlete to achieve his or her potential, no matter what that might be.'

NATIONAL AGENCIES

Historically, successive governments of all political persuasions have directly and indirectly influenced sports development in the UK. Initially the development of health and fitness was the main aim, ensuring a constant supply of manpower for industry and war. In the 1930s the Central Council of Physical Education (CCPR) was set up to act as a forum for the various sports governing bodies and influence physical education in schools. It was during the same period that an improved syllabus for physical education was introduced into state schools. During the post-Second World War period, as the economy and international political tensions eased, individual sports evolved.

In 1972 Denis Howell, himself a football referee, was appointed the first Minister for Sport. His first task was to set up the Sports Councils for England, Scotland, Wales and Northern Ireland and an umbrella UK coordinating body. One of their priorities was to identify and oversee national centres throughout the UK for a variety of sports. In simple terms the role of the various Sports Councils was to encourage the development of sporting opportunities and facilities throughout the regions, and fund individual sports and events. One of their early projects was the Sport for All campaign which was aimed at getting more people involved in sport and physical activity. Working with the CCPR, the SC has increased the provision and resourcing for participation for all ages and all abilities from local leisure centres to national and international competitions.

As the nature and structure of society have evolved, and leisure time and disposable income have increased, these national agencies have kept pace with changes. Recently the Sports Council has reinvented itself as Sport England, Sport Northern Ireland, Sport Scotland, Sport Wales, and the supreme body, Sport UK. To meet changing demands they have introduced a structure of funding for individual sports and facilities at national, regional and local level; introduced a national coaching framework; created various agencies to identify talent and performance development, and strengthened links with international sports organisations.

The philosophy of Sport UK has been implemented by a range of specialised sub-units to:

- increase levels of participation – Sport for All
- develop strategies to increase the opportunities for social inclusion within sport
- assess current resources and assess future needs
- monitor the provision of specialised sporting facilities
- develop strategies for greater use of existing facilities
- build new facilities

- identify talent and develop performance
- develop training opportunities and associated coach education programmes
- implement regional planning
- boost the opportunities for national and international competition for athletes
- utilise National Lottery funding to provide financial support for athletes
- implement anti-dope procedures
- foster the development of related research
- provide and develop opportunities for careers in sport.

POLITICAL PERSPECTIVES

Though there are many organisations that contribute to a 'national framework', and one could argue that the government directly and indirectly controls or influences them all, especially financially, it would be naïve to believe that there are no specific central government agendas. These seem to be:

- A healthy population makes fewer demands on the National Health Service, thereby reducing the cost of medical care.
- Physical education as part of the National Curriculum contributes to the overall education of the young.
- Physical activity provides a means for social inclusion, which helps general interaction between individuals and groups and ensures integration for all social groupings.
- National sport gives the country a sense of patriotism and pride. Such a feel-good factor following the 1966 World Cup, according to Harold Wilson, helped the government of the day to be re-elected.
- Encourages healthy competition as countries strive to make their planning, preparation and running of major events better than any other country's.

- Provides a vehicle for low-level political disapproval on the world stage, e.g. Margaret Thatcher's wish that British sportsmen and women should boycott the 1980 Olympic Games.
- To make an international statement that a nation's political system produces champions and is therefore better than others. The old East Germany was a classic example of this policy, but even they pale into insignificance compared with Nazi Germany.

A FINANCIAL DIMENSION

There is no doubt as to the very important part that sport plays in modern society for both the participants and the spectators. Sport is big business. Television, newspapers, radio and the internet apportion a great deal of space, time and resources. The distinctions between amateurism and professionalism are now barely visible. Sports which exist under either or both structures offer lucrative careers for the successful few. Salaries of millions of pounds a year, celebrity status, a host of sponsors and promoters wishing to endorse a sport or an individual are commonplace. Professional football as an example immediately springs to mind, as do rugby, cricket and athletics. It has long been suggested that in high-profile Olympic sports, such as track and field or swimming, a gold medal is worth at least £1,000,000 with the right marketing and product endorsement. Career and financial opportunities in sport as players, coaches, sports scientists, managers, agents, journalists, commentators and pundits are all part of a booming industry.

How might a philosophy emerge from these various elements? For the player: 'An opportunity for sporting ability to provide a financially lucrative career.' For the others? 'An opportunity to market sports and their participants in a mutually advantageous financial manner.'

With so many different considerations, and I am sure that there are many others, the process of coaching champions is not only complicated but sometimes downright confusing. Though it might be argued that all the organisations involved are pulling in the same direction, it might well be that at least part of their influence has an edge more of self-interest than of altruism. All parents want the best for their children and for the talented youngster they might see sport as a lucrative career opportunity. By encouraging their youngsters they are giving them every opportunity to succeed. But overenthusiasm; pushing them too hard too soon; being overcritical or too demanding; having unrealistic expectations;

achieving status and recognition for being the parents of a star performer, or even trying to make up for their own lack of opportunity or success through their children can cloud the underlying process. One of the drawbacks of this situation can be that children think that if they do not meet their parents' levels of expectation they have failed them, and feel desperately guilty. The young athlete has enough problems associated with maturation without being overloaded with other people's. More often than not some or all of these pressures result in rapid deterioration in performance in both the short and long term.

Schools do provide an opportunity for the development of competence but they too can exert unnecessary pressure. Teachers, officially or unofficially, are often rated by the success of their pupils, and this can influence promotion prospects. There is a whole series of league tables that compare schools with national standards and examinations. Often this is part of the process by which parents select schools. The success of sports teams and individuals reflects well on the school and creates a favourable reputation. With funding from national agencies schools can now achieve recognition for sporting prowess and receive funding to build extensive sports facilities. Obviously this will have an impact on the quality of experience for all pupils within timetabled lessons and extra-curricular sessions. Not only does this situation give added acknowledgement to the school's achievements but enables the local community to share in the success by using the upgraded resources.

National governing bodies exist to provide opportunities for the whole community at all levels. The amount of money they receive from national agencies, sponsorship or other sources is finite; they have to prioritise spending. This can mean that specific areas from time to time will be favoured with sufficient funding while others are not. For example, if moneys are directed towards increasing international success with the current squads, as may happen in preparations for an Olympic Games, it may be drawn away from the grassroots. Funding can be as a result of a particular emphasis on a sport, proportional to the number of participants or as recognition for national or international success. But obviously any success in major international events will improve the chances of gaining additional income. The difficulty arises if it is attracted only by elite performance because then the process that brings talent through will be compromised.

Coaches, like teachers, are often appraised on the success of the athletes they coach. Many coaches see themselves as part of the local club establishment and relish their work. But those who aspire to higher levels and recognition within the sport may see that promotion is a result of focusing on those elite individuals who have the potential to be champions. The players who fail to meet the standard are quickly relegated in favour of up-and-coming talent. Both philosophies have merit and both must be accommodated if the structure by which talent can progress is to be established.

As a supernational agency, Sport UK has to enable all sports to develop and flourish in their own way. It has, on one hand, to attempt to resource all its disparate responsibilities in a Sport For All context enabling each individual to achieve the level of participation commensurate with his or her talent and inclination; and on the other, to meet all its targets of participation and increased standards of performance and international success as evidence that it has spent government money – our money – wisely. An unenviable position!

Financial demands can place other pressures on players. Sponsors and the media want to see sport of the very highest quality at all times. Demands on performers can pressure them into using performance-enhancing drugs to maintain the required standards. An individual with some celebrity status may have to play in a game despite injury because the sponsors need to endorse their product by means of a winning performance. No company wants to be associated with a failed team or star. It has been alleged that sponsors of individual players and teams have influenced selection at national level to obtain a return for their investment.

Coaching champions is a minefield; figure 1.1 shows the range of personnel and resources that all of those involved need to consider. There are as many personal agendas as those who participate, in whatever capacity. There is a place for everyone even if at times it might be a little difficult to see where! But, in all of this there is one factor that should not be overlooked. Coaching champions can bring many benefits for all those involved in sport – but what about the individuals concerned? What is their agenda? What do they want to do? What are their aspirations? As the following chapters demonstrate, potential champions having all the qualities to achieve the greatest heights can still be vulnerable to the influence of those around them. At different stages in their development youngsters will be exposed to those with priorities that might conflict with their own. In the interests of all concerned, especially the athlete, in the short and long term enthusiasm may have to be tempered with caution.

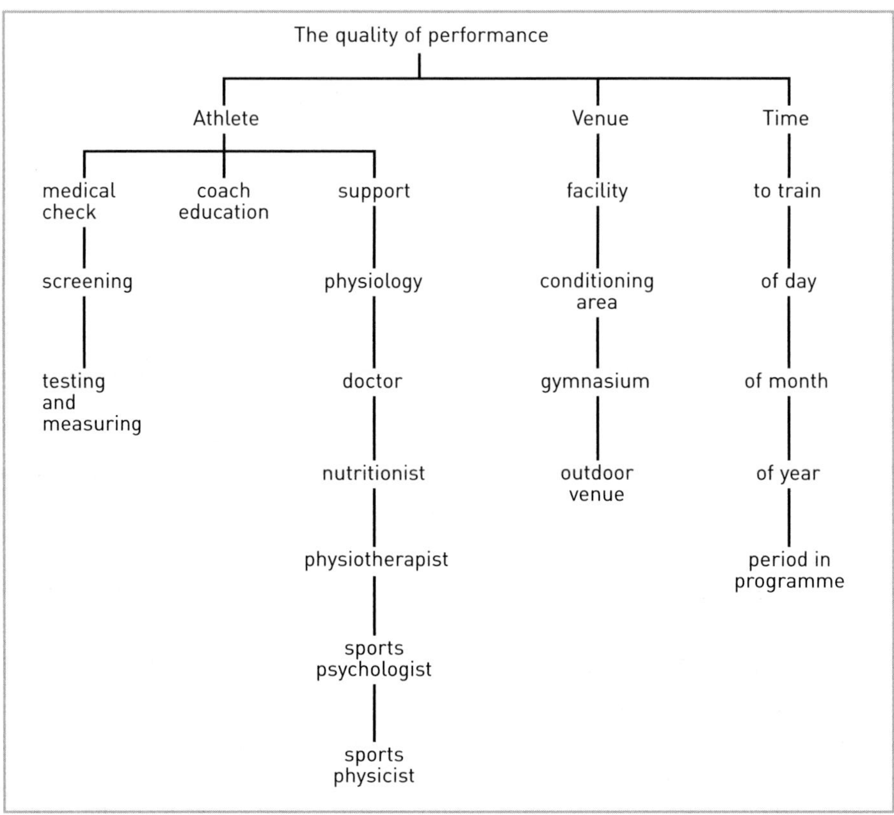

FIG. 1.1 Performance development involves many people and contributory factors. The degree to which these are present or utilised will affect an athlete's rate of learning and their ultimate achievement.

CHAPTER 2
IDENTIFYING POTENTIAL TALENT

Throughout early life, play in some form or other is an essential feature of personal and social activity. Physical activity is an opportunity for individuals to develop practical, intellectual, behavioural and social skills which will improve the quality of their life during their childhood and prepare them for adulthood. Participating in informal play or organised sport can account for a large part of the day for children and adolescents. In terms of current and future health and sporting opportunities, the impact of participation in physical activity during this period cannot be underestimated.

It is only natural that parents and guardians want their children to achieve success in all aspects of their lives including leisure interests. Parents like to see their children succeed in sport as part of that involvement. There are those who have the desire to see their youngster achieve success now and at all stages up to and including international levels. It is perceived by some that a process of talent identification and selective performance development is part of that process. Currently the methodology of identifying potential is ad hoc, relying on subjective assessment by those concerned. What is now being suggested is a much more formal identification and selection of youngsters displaying the appropriate physical, intellectual and behavioural sport-specific qualities.

It is vital that from the very start of such a selection process clear guidelines are set down to ensure that talent is nurtured and developed, but far more importantly that the interests and safety of the developing athlete are paramount in the planning and decision-making processes. Children by definition are not mature, and are vulnerable to the pressures placed on them by adults. These demands might be totally honourable and emerge as a genuine enthusiasm for their development and success. However, there are those who would seek to exploit young talent for their own ends and purposes. The youngster has to be protected from overzealousness from whatever quarter. These issues will be dealt with in following chapters.

But suppose a youngster displays talent, and suppose various tests and measures indicate that she or he has the potential to be an elite gymnast but prefers basketball! They may later in life become a reasonably proficient basketball player who enjoys recreational and club involvement and obtains great personal satisfaction from their playing. But, if they had been convinced or coerced into training and competing in gymnastics they could possibly have been an Olympic champion. The question is, whose needs are best served? The youngster who wants to play and enjoy basketball as a fun thing to do, or everyone else who sees their own agendas being addressed at the expense of the individual?

It could be argued that it is in the long-term sporting interest of the child to be 'directed' by expert opinion, and that the child's immaturity is such that adults should make decisions for them. Certainly, this was the case in former Eastern bloc countries where parents saw the success of the child as an opportunity for a better standard of living for themselves and an escape from the deprivations and drudgery of everyday life. In a totalitarian state the interests of the national good are paramount and in every way outweigh the needs of the individual. They become a dispensable vehicle for national aspirations. Their welfare and future life, especially after they have outlived their sporting usefulness, are of no consequence.

In a 'free' society an individual can make choices. Should those who display talent in one sport be allowed to play another? What degree of 'direction' should adults give in influencing youngsters? When should importance be given to the wishes of the youngster? It would seem that sporting talent in the UK finds its correct outlet by chance, serendipity. The right people meet at the right place at the right time. It may seem like a considerable waste of talent but at least most of those involved are happy!

But there are countries who see this process of talent identification in almost clinical terms. The ideas of the Eastern Bloc are alive and well and are still implemented to various degrees in countries around the world. It is alleged that Cuba and China are the clearest examples. Indeed, many of the coaches from the old Eastern bloc work throughout the world, including in the West, and still support such values. Which is an interesting notion when one wonders whatever happened to the vast majority of those athletes screened who failed the selection process? Did they continue participating in sport? Were they allowed to, or were limited resources made available only to the elite few?

TESTING

The East German model identifies two periods in the maturation and assessment process:

Period 1: Age Range 3–8 Years

Around the onset of the first growth spurt selected children undergo a medical examination carried out by a paediatrician with a specialism in sports medicine. A thorough check of the anatomical and physiological systems is made to detect any conditions which would have a negative influence on performance. Assessments of motor skills, predicted physique and coachability are undertaken, and even at this stage individuals are directed to specific sports such as swimming, gymnastics or diving. Predictions of mature height can be made using radiological measurements of bones and comparing these with standard data. Since only specialised and expensive procedures can do this an alternative is to assess the height of parents and from standard charts estimate future physique. Obviously being tall is an important factor in basketball, volleyball or high-jumping while a smaller stature is advantageous in gymnastics and diving. It is suggested that this initial assessment is essential in the development of talent since it directs resources to those individuals with the sport-specific potential. In countries with limited resources this process enables them to derive maximum success from their restricted means.

Training during this period is focused on the development and refinement of general and sport-specific skills; integrating visual perception and movement; reaction training and generalised conditioning, progressively developing speed of movement; aerobic endurance; suppleness and relative strength by using the athlete's own bodyweight as the resistance. Training sessions should be gradually increased in frequency to at least three per week. This 'foundation training phase' has been identified as the most important period in performance development.

Period 2: Age Range 9–17 Years

This second stage selection process is by its very nature applied to those youngsters who have been subjected to intensive general and sport-specific preparation. Testing at this stage will identify those *crème de la crème* who will be selected for further specialised and intensive training in what was known as the 'build-up' phase. Assessment is based on achieving physique indicators and targets in speed, strength, skill, suppleness and stamina, however at this stage competition is deemed to be the best indication of potential. Allowances are made for the early onset of puberty in girls of 9–14 and boys of 12–17 years, figure 2.1 shows the effect of puberty on growth during this period. It is not until after puberty that sports which require intensive strength, speed and stamina training, such as weight lifting, shot-putting and rowing, make their final selection. The intensity of training and workloads should be increasing throughout the period, especially in the final two years. The number of training sessions should be increasing to at least six per week at the end. Competitions or fixtures should be increasing in number and in quality.

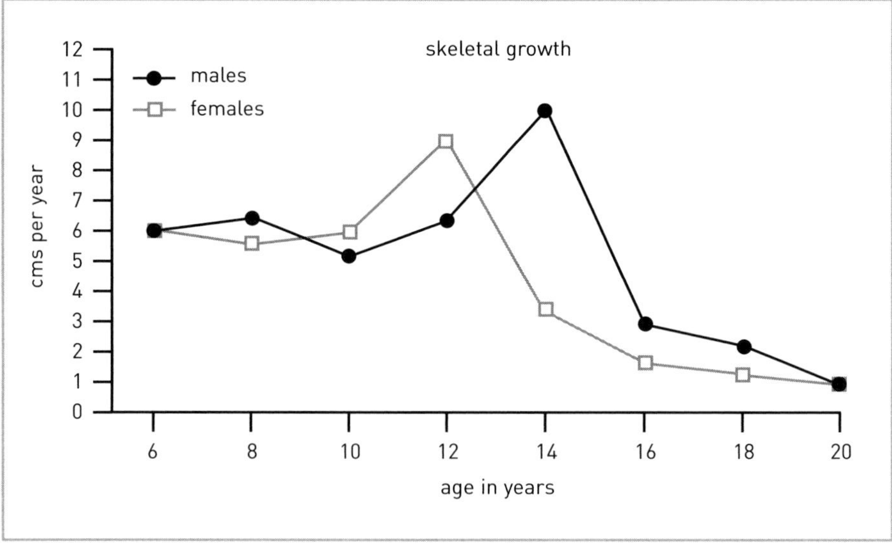

FIG. 2.1 The difference in times and rates of growth between boys and girls can be clearly seen.

Period 3: Age Range 17 Years On

Training is gearing up to mature intensities to match the demands of elite-level sport. The intensity and number of training sessions increases.

Any such process of talent identification is not just evaluation of sporting qualities. At each and every stage individuals have to be compared with target scores produced by the specific sport. And, with team games such as football, selection protocols are detailed enough to identify special qualities for individual positions.

In the former German Democratic Republic (DDR) this process included a primary school physical education programme to identify potential talent, and sports clubs only for gifted children. Ruthless selection tests were imposed by selected sports schools and sport-specific schools for the elite. Out of a population of almost 20,000,000 people 80,000 potential and actual champions were coached in specialised facilities by 10,000 full-time coaches. If champions are made and not born then this was a structure to do just that! If this situation were transferred to the present UK of almost 60,000,000 people, 240,000 possibly elite athletes would be coached by 30,000 full-time coaches! That is a situation that all national governing bodies of sport and related government departments might wish to consider.

TALENT DEVELOPMENT IN THE UNITED KINGDOM

Recent national agency statistics produce an interesting comparison with the much-praised Eastern Bloc model. In the UK it is estimated that there are over 4,000,000 children in school served by the National Curriculum for Physical Education which is delivered by some 20,000 specialist teachers. A close examination of the National Curriculum for Physical Education particularly in Key Stages 1 and 2 displays a very close comparison to the skill development of the DDR. The sequential development of skills is related to the physical and mental development of the maturing youngster.

The main difference in the UK lies in the fact that the Eastern bloc model took the children out of school to receive intensive training from sport-specialist coaches and that the pool of schoolchildren served only as a reservoir of potential to be identified and nurtured. In the UK, to all intents and purposes the same developmental process is undertaken within the schools. Unfortunately the number of specialist primary physical education teachers trained to implement such activity is limited. There was a national policy to train such specialists but along with other educational innovations it was shelved in the name of pedagogical and social progress!

The second difficulty with the physical experience of youngsters is the demand made upon the school curriculum by other subject areas. Schools have to meet national targets for literacy and specified academic and scientific subjects. Heads and teachers are under a great deal of pressure to ensure that pupils achieve the necessary grades which are published in national and local tables. The very existence of schools and related teaching posts can depend on good scores and reviews. In such a climate it is self-evident that parts of the curriculum can be squeezed and less space allocated on the timetable. When heads have to make a decision on appointing new staff it is clear that they are influenced by the academic needs of the pupils and the school.

The situation in secondary schools is a little better in that there are specialist teachers of physical education but there are considerable pressures on the actual amount of time allocated for physical education lessons and games – less than two hours a week! Youngsters are guided, through the curriculum, to continue the development of general skills but now there is a subtle shift in emphasis through Key Stage 3 and the refinement of modified games skills to specific ones in Key Stage 4. Pupils are encouraged to specialise in individual games in the post-16 years, eventually identifying an individual sport for continued development.

Running parallel to Key Stages 1, 2, 3 and 4 are the national governing bodies' development programmes for their sport. Though schools offer opportunities for the development of talent through clubs and teams they often create links with local clubs and coaches enabling aspiring champions to develop even more. All physical educationalists realise that when young champions or enthusiastic recreational players leave school the only avenue for them is through the national governing body. Such organisations provide the opportunity for recreational, leisure and performance development to the highest levels.

This strategy is generally delivered at a local level through clubs and coaches. It is suggested that there are 6.5 million members of 150,000 sports clubs in the UK. It would be safe to assume that some members are former players, friends and family with a social association, and not actually active participants. There are, of course, many young members, who finding an interest in sport, seek to develop it in the governing body setting. Servicing these players is an army of 200,000 voluntary coaches and 500,000 officials. Sports Coach UK, Sport

England's 'coaching arm', claimed in 2001 to have in excess of 10,000 registered coaches. As to the number of full-time sports coaches appointed by national governing bodies it would be fair to suggest that there are fewer than 1,000 which is hardly a centrally coordinated strategy.

The boundaries of operation of sports coaches and physical education, once extremely well defined, have recently become more vague. The new range of governing body coaching awards, together with police screening, has created qualifications that have national recognition and acceptance. Specialist coaches are now able to work in the schools without additional teaching qualifications. Indeed, many schools employ coaches to develop specific sports or activities that might be outside the experience of the PE teacher. These links not only benefit the physical experience of the pupils but create a natural bridge between schools and clubs. With the lack of specialists in primary schools, very often coaches and parents with coaching awards are major contributors to the sporting opportunities. There are philosophical and pedagogical issues that surround such situations but suffice it to say this is an area that many national agencies seek to develop.

Coaching

An interesting item of research came out of the DDR programme that related to coaches. It compared the sporting background of coaches to their seniority in the coaching structure. The lower levels of coaching, 1 and 2, tend to be delivered by individuals who have a limited background in the sport. Many have no playing experience while others have school, club or college involvement. As one examines the higher levels of coaching, 3, 4 and above, it becomes apparent that the coaches themselves have played the game at national and international levels. Anecdotally there are those who will achieve success without having a career in sport, but they are a small minority. As an example, if one looks at managers and coaches in the premier divisions of football in the UK and Europe, most are ex-international players.

The DDR model focused on the ex-player with a great knowledge and understanding of the sport and its underpinning skills as the mechanism for talent exploitation. Interestingly, in the UK, following the Athens Olympics, there has been a call from national agencies to encourage elite athletes to become active in going into clubs and schools not just to give the sport a high profile but to be

involved in the coaching of potential champions. Once again this mirrors the East German example.

The DDR model created a situation where former athletes, now coaches, having gone through the process themselves were deemed to have the additional insight into what makes a champion. Similarly they were ruthless in identifying those who did not have the potential.

The skills of coaching with regard to planning, preparation, delivery, assessment and review are critical in the transfer and development of knowledge and understanding. The range of personal attributes required are extensive, going far beyond the technical to include:

- appearance
- enthusiasm
- ability to motivate
- use of voice
- use of appropriate language
- explanation
- demonstration
- personal conduct.

It is not within the limitations of this book to explore beyond an outline of the skills of coaching. However, it can be seen that such qualities are long in the developing. Whereas the physical education teacher has a long training process of four years or more to hone these qualities, the preparation for coaches is at best abbreviated. This might be the root cause of a core issue, the autocratic 'style' of coaching.

In academic circles there is much debate as to the difference between coaching and teaching. My experience is that there is none. They are both on the pedagogical continuum along with many other aspects such as training, instructing and advising. Though subtly different, all are part of the communicator's repertoire. However, there are quite distinct considerations between what might be considered the performance and personal development strategies.

To a significant degree governing bodies have as part of their remit a talent identification and performance development structure. Elite performance reflects well on a sport in terms of recognition, prestige and associated increases in income. It might be argued that the success of the few enables the governing body to provide for the remainder! That is a view that I would not entirely subscribe to. The very ethos of such a structure is providing resources for the elite. With such a system those who may never achieve or are no longer at the very pinnacle of success must make way for those who are up and coming. This is reflected in the style of coaching adopted.

The American sociologist Amitai Etzioni suggested that in society there were three systems of organisation:

- autocracy – absolute government by one person
- democracy – an egalitarian form of government
- laissez-faire – no governmental interference.

Wilf Paish, the internationally acknowledged athletics coach, encapsulated this theory in his view of coaching:

- Do as I say! (Autocratic) – I am the expert, you are the novice. I have the knowledge and ability to enable you to achieve success. If you follow exactly the programme I present, you will be a champion. In the early stages of a coach–athlete relationship novices have little or no knowledge of the sport or what is required to achieve success. If they are to succeed they must follow exactly and achieve what the coach demands.
- Let's discuss it! (Democratic) – after several years of working with a coach the athlete has been through several training programmes and countless different sessions and has developed a good understanding of the demands of the sport and training requirements. The coach and athlete can now discuss training and competitive strategies from a mutual understanding of what works best. A collaborative situation is achieved.
- If you have any problems contact me! – after many years of working together the athlete knows much more about the sport and preparation and is perfectly able to work on his or her own. But there are always going to be difficulties and these are the times when the athlete seeks the help and advice of the coach.

It can take many years to work through the levels!

More recently Sports Coach UK, formerly the National Coaching Foundation, Sport England's coaching arm, produced a similar structure, as have eminent American coaches. It can be seen that the focus of this style of coaching is performance. The Eastern Bloc countries adopted this format. Coaching was totally autocratic, success was everything. The athlete as a person was fourth or fifth down the list of priorities. This dictatorial style is arguably the most effective when dealing with young athletes. No discussion – do it! Since the removal of the Iron Curtain many coaches who worked on the performance development programmes have delivered workshops in the UK. For many of us who have attended such sessions the demands made by the coach on the athlete and the 'rigorous' training environment have been eye-opening, to say the least. But that system, despite its implications, seems to work.

However, there is another perspective of improvement: personal development. Progress is related to an individual's ability and inclination. This is the educationalist perspective. The physical educationalist in schools has to address the issue of dealing with a range of abilities and degrees of commitment to physical activity in every lesson, 'differentiation' and 'inclusion'. They have to devise strategies that will engage and challenge everyone. The ultimate standard of performance is not the aim. The single most important consideration is the individual. All activity is child-centred, based upon their potential and aspirations. With such an aim in mind an autocratic strategy is inappropriate. The PE teacher has to adopt different styles of operation, often within one lesson. These might include:

- formal information – health and safety issues
- personal practice – working on their own
- working in small groups – coaching each other
- working through skill tests – comparing with others
- deciding what activity to practise – and what role they will have
- accepting responsibility for their own actions
- discovering different or new ways of doing things
- problem solving.

The thought of pupils taking control of their own development would be an anathema to the DDR model. But in this pedagogical format physical education is used as a means of personal development and socialisation. Any sporting improvement is a bonus! This is a simplistic perception but it serves to identify the aims and objectives within physical education and the National Curriculum.

It would appear that in the UK the systems are in place, the resources are there for each and every youngster to participate in physical activity to whatever level they wish. What seems to be different from the DDR exemplar is a basic philosophy. In the Eastern Bloc model the youngster is directed without choice to the sport for which they have the necessary potential. This talent is then exploited on a conveyor belt of physical and human resources. Success is paramount. The needs of the individual are of little concern. In the UK and I suspect the west in general, individuals have choices to play sport or not. And, if they choose to, they decide which sport they want to play. It might well be, and often is, that their potential and ability is not best suited to the activity of their choice. But they enjoy playing it, and may achieve a fair measure of success – but not as much as if they had taken up the sport for which they had potential.

It might well be argued that for an individual to achieve success in sport in the UK or the west it is by serendipity, fortuitous happenstance, luck! I suspect in many cases that is the reality. But what is the alternative – to force youngsters to play a sport against their will, where those adults in positions of authority or control feel it is in the best interests of the child? What seems to be happening in the UK is that more organisations are seeking to select talent at an ever-earlier age so that it can be groomed. That did not happen in the DDR!

I have never 'coached' a youngster under the age of 16 years. I want athletes to take up a sport because they want to. Wilf Paish has a similar philosophy. And, in a recent interview on television, Sir Alec Ferguson stated that he would coach young players who were over 16. But it depends what you mean by coaching! The general consensus would tend to define it as 'systematic and intensive preparation for the competitive situation'. Any such activity is inappropriate for an under-16-year-old, physically and mentally. But what is appropriate, and what all coaches would support, is a more enjoyable, less serious yet structured exposure to the skills and modified competition structure of an activity, which will lead on to the more intensive phase should the athlete wish.

There is some mileage in the suggestion that the later you start a sport the longer you will stay in it and consequently the better you will become. This addresses issues relating to boredom and burn-out curtailing participation in the mid-teens. If one looks at sports that have an age-related competition structure it is rare that a talented player is at the top at, say, under 7, 8, 9, 10, 11, 12, 13, 14, 15, 16, 17, 18, 19, 20 and into the senior ranks. Often those who show ability in the early years drop out for a variety of reasons. It is more the case that those who emerge in the post-16 and even later stages move on to elite status. The difficulty is that the occasional precocious individual will emerge as with Tiger Woods, but that is the exception not the rule.

The long-held guidance given to coaches and teachers is to delay intensive training until after puberty when mental and physical maturation has achieved a measure of stability. This is a perception with which the medical profession, exercise physiologists, teachers, coaches and other interested parties would concur. However despite the wealth of evidence there have been suggestions that this might not be the best policy. It has been suggested that intensive training does not pose a difficulty. I would counsel anyone coaching a young athlete not to see that as a green light. 'One swallow does not make a summer'; the findings of an isolated researcher which stand against a wealth of contradictory evidence must be regarded with a degree of circumspection, especially in view of the knowledge that the health and welfare of the youngster is paramount, now and in the future.

It is clearly evident that the UK has a complicated delivery structure for sport. However it encompasses all that is identified as best practice in providing opportunities for participation at whatever level, in a wide range of activities, and has a structure for talent identification and performance development. There is ample scope for a measure of integration and pooling of resources and expertise, and there is great merit and potential in the organisations that exist to do so. The DDR model and the UK/Western one in a sporting context are very similar and offer an almost identical process for performance development. However they are politically, philosophically and culturally at odds with each other when it comes to the democratic process and free choice.

Interestingly, it is suggested that Australia, an internationally acclaimed sporting nation, has followed a modified talent identification and performance development programme along the lines of the former DDR with a fair measure of success in specific activities. The selection process through the schools system has identified talent in similar manner. Resources have been directed towards the elite few, and those who do not continue to meet the constant review criteria are asked to leave the programme. But, there are now some who have serious reservations as to the underpinning philosophy of such a programme and the lack of resources being made available for the greater majority who do not warrant such special attention.

To reinforce this strategic review there are suggestions that the Chinese desire to achieve sporting success, especially with the forthcoming Beijing Olympics in 2008, is producing similar concerns. Young sportsmen and women who have failed in the system and been cast aside are realising that they have sacrificed their education and childhood to the dream of medals and are now ill prepared for adult life. With no occupational or vocational training their futures seem less than glowing. Many are seeking to utilise their sporting experiences by attending Western universities, particularly in the USA and UK. There are those in China who are beginning to identify the failings of their established coaching systems and are seeking a more child-centred approach. Indeed many now realise that future sporting success need not necessarily require such a high price to be paid.

Perhaps we should not throw out the baby with the bathwater: the British system has much to commend it, warts and all!

Talent Identification

During the developmental phases of both the DDR and NCPE models, skills are taught and developed in a systematic and progressive manner. I have, over the years, developed a series of tests that are based upon these generic skills. Obviously at some point in a session the individual activities are taught as activities in their own right as the coach may decide. But, by occasionally setting time aside, youngsters can have a go, in an enjoyable and convivial environment, at working through the test lists under the watchful eye of the coach who can monitor the degree of competence shown. At the end of a session time might be planned for fun activity, and these assessments could occasionally be used in this period.

The results of such activity serves several purposes. It identifies:

- if a youngster can perform a skill – if not the matter needs to be rectified by modification of future lessons
- the quality of movement
- the repeatability of a skill by intention not chance
- if the general training regime is achieving its aims

- areas of particular emphasis before progressing to the next phase. Since more complex movements are based upon a foundation of well-rehearsed simple ones, safety issues require that all previous phases need to be mastered, and this must govern the rate of progress.

My suggestion is the youngsters work through part of a list, say, ten exercises one session and the rest the next. Working through a complete list might be the skill-development part of the session itself. Coaches can mix and match as they see fit. But, more importantly, coaches can and should devise their own lists! There is a plethora of sequential core skills that are encapsulated in governing body training and assessment guidelines. The following examples of skill drills and tests serve as a guideline to the type of activities that can be included. But, of course you, the coach, are the one with the sport-specific knowledge and the abilities to modify activities and devise your own. The critical factor is that they fit into the sequential maturational and motor development phases. There is no issue with coaches making the generic skills sport-specific at the appropriate developmental level.

Test 1

1. Guerilla crawl
2. Hands and knees crawl
3. Seal walk
4. Crouch walk
5. Bear walk
6. Crab walk
7. Walk
8. Run
9. Sprint
10. Run and stop with both feet together
11. Run and stop on left foot
12. Run and stop on right foot
13. Run between cones
14. Hop
15. Giant strides

COACHING TIP
All of the exercises from 7 onwards are probably best assessed with the athlete moving down a line. This will enable the correct movement to be monitored and any rotation or unwanted actions to be noted.

Test 2

1. Run, jump and land – with bent knees
2. Run, jump take off with right foot, land on both feet
3. Run, jump take off with right foot, land on right foot
4. Run, jump take off with right foot, land on left foot
5. Run, jump take off with left foot, land on both feet
6. Run, jump take off with left foot, land on left foot
7. Run, jump take off with left foot, land on right foot
8. Run, jump, stretch and land
9. Run, jump, tuck and land
10. Run, jump, half turn and land
11. Run, jump, full turn and land
12. Continuous hop on left foot
13. Continuous hop on right foot
14. Continuous steps (giant strides)
15. Continuous two footed jumps

COACHING TIP
Once again a line on the floor can be used to help assess control and co-ordination.

Test Three

1. Kipper roll left
2. Kipper roll right
3. Forward roll – to crouch
4. Forward roll – to stand
5. Forward roll from half squat position – to crouch
6. Dive forward roll from standing
7. Backward roll – to crouch

8 Backward roll – to stand
9 Backward roll from half squat position – to crouch
10 Side roll left
11 Side roll right
12 Diagonal roll front left
13 Diagonal roll front right
14 Diagonal roll back left
15 Diagonal roll back right

COACHING TIP
Practise these activities only with mats that are approved for gymnastics.

Test Four

1 Throw, both hands high right
2 Throw, both hands high centre
3 Throw, both hands high left
4 Throw, both hands waist-level right
5 Throw, both hands waist-level centre
6 Throw, both hands waist-level left
7 Throw, both hands low right
8 Throw, both hands low centre
9 Throw, both hands low left
10 Throw, high right, right hand
11 Throw, high centre, right hand
12 Throw, high left, right hand
13 Throw, waist-level right, right hand
14 Throw, waist-level centre, right hand
15 Throw, waist-level left, right hand
16 Throw, low right, right hand
17 Throw, low centre, right hand
18 Throw, low left, right hand
19 Throw, high right, left hand
20 Throw, high centre, left hand
21 Throw, high left, left hand

22 Throw, waist-level right, left hand
23 Throw, waist-level centre, left hand
24 Throw, waist-level left, left hand
25 Throw, low right, left hand
26 Throw, low centre, left hand
27 Throw, low left, left hand
28 Overhead throw both hands, feet side by side (football throw-in)
29 Overhead throw both hands, left foot forward
30 Overhead throw both hands, right foot forward

COACHING TIP
The size of the ball can be varied to change the difficulty of the tests. The correct ball for the sport should be used, but not all the time. A partner or the coach can be the receiver/feeder.

Test Five

1 Catch, both hands high right
2 Catch, both hands high centre
3 Catch, both hands high left
4 Catch, both hands waist-level right
5 Catch, both hands waist-level centre
6 Catch, both hands waist-level left
7 Catch, both hands low right
8 Catch, both hands low centre
9 Catch, both hands low left
10 Catch, high right, right hand
11 Catch, high centre, right hand
12 Catch, high left, right hand
13 Catch, waist-level right, right hand
14 Catch, waist-level centre, right hand
15 Catch, waist-level left, right hand
16 Catch, low right, right hand
17 Catch, low centre, right hand
18 Catch, low left, right hand

19 Catch, high right, left hand
20 Catch, high centre, left hand
21 Catch, high left, left hand
22 Catch, waist-level right, left hand
23 Catch, waist-level centre, left hand
24 Catch, waist-level left, left hand
25 Catch, low right, left hand
26 Catch, low centre, left hand
27 Catch, low left, left hand
28 Jump to catch both hands
29 Jump to catch right hand
30 Jump to catch left hand

COACHING TIP
The size of the ball can be varied to change the difficulty of the tests. The correct ball for the sport should be used, but not all the time. A partner or the coach can be the feeder.

Test Six

1 Bat, both hands high right
2 Bat, both hands high centre
3 Bat, both hands high left
4 Bat, both hands waist-level right
5 Bat, both hands waist-level centre
6 Bat, both hands waist-level left
7 Bat, both hands low right
8 Bat, both hands low centre
9 Bat, both hands low left
10 Bat, high right, right hand
11 Bat, high centre, right hand
12 Bat, high left, right hand
13 Bat, waist-level right, right hand
14 Bat, waist-level centre, right hand
15 Bat, waist-level left, right hand

16 Bat, low right, right hand
17 Bat, low centre, right hand
18 Bat, low left, right hand
19 Bat, high right, left hand
20 Bat, high centre, left hand
21 Bat, high left, left hand
22 Bat, waist-level right, left hand
23 Bat, waist-level centre, left hand
24 Bat, waist-level left, left hand
25 Bat, low right, left hand
26 Bat, low centre, left hand
27 Bat, low left, left hand
28 Jump to bat, both hands
29 Jump to bat, right hand
30 Jump to bat, left hand

COACHING TIP

The size and type of racket or bat can be varied to change the difficulty of the tests. The correct type of racket or bat can be used, but not all the time. A partner or the coach can be a feeder/receiver.

CHAPTER 3
AGES FOR STAGES OF SKILL DEVELOPMENT

AN OVERVIEW

Sports were predominantly devised by men for men at the peak of their physical and mental condition (figure 3.1). Some evolved as a stylised form of military training and combat as a preparation for war while others evolved out of the primitive urge to compete against others in various situations such as trials of strength, agility and skill. One therefore has to look at the appropriateness of such activities for the young, the old and those of a less robust nature! The relevance of adult sports and training practices and their impact on immature bodies and

FIG. 3.1 The age at which most sportsmen and women achieve sporting success at international levels is between 20 and 30 years.

minds needs careful monitoring and consideration. The paradox of early identification of talent and the need to nurture and develop it are seen by many as the key to success in sport and of sport for the benefit of the country and the individuals concerned. But from the very outset it has to be acknowledged throughout the process that, 'Children are not little adults!'

As a more enlightened approach to the situation has developed there has been an upsurge in research into the importance and effect of physical activity on the developing youngster. Unfortunately what has often been produced are programmes of training and skill development for adults which have been 'watered down' for young athletes and are totally inappropriate (figure 3.2). However, out of these studies has emerged a generalised pattern of motor and specific skill learning. These patterns reflect the parallel in physical and intellectual growth in the maturational process, which are interwoven in any general or specific action or technique. It therefore follows that there has to be a carefully designed programme of training which corresponds with the development level of the individual.

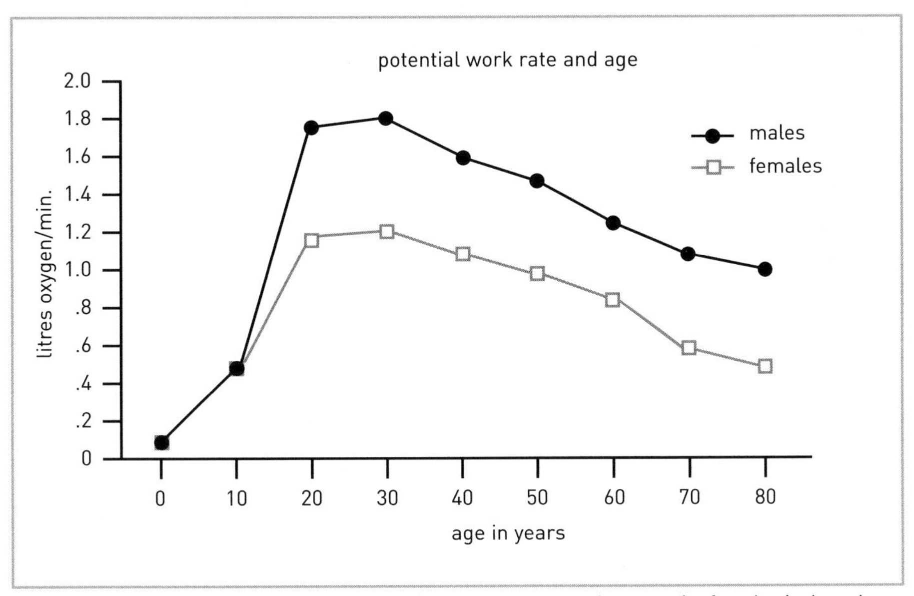

FIG. 3.2 Using maximum oxygen consumption as a measure, the capacity for physical work peaks in the period from 20 to 30 years of age.

MOTOR LEARNING

There is evidence to support the notion of four broad and progressive areas of skill development.

Reflex Movements

From birth and even, according to some experts, before birth, the individual is evolving basic reflex-type movements. These tend to be basic postural movements, especially of the head, neck and back as well as tentative movements of the limbs by flexing and extending joints. The infant is generally exploring its body and the ability to interact with the immediate surroundings. As sight, hearing, touch and balance improve, along with developments in physical and intellectual capacity, more demanding skills are performed, such as sitting, reaching, grasping, crawling, standing and walking. These more advanced skills in turn allow the infant to experience more stimuli from the world around and create the foundation for further intellectual and physical growth. It is generally accepted that this level of attainment is achieved when the individual is about 2 years old, although to stick rigidly to chronological age can be misleading as some youngsters will obviously develop at a more rapid rate than others.

The developing individual needs the opportunity to experience these basic movements. The more the stimulation the greater will be potential for these skills to be practised and refined. Obviously the parents and family are a vital part of this phase which is extremely important since the next area of skill development is built on this one. It therefore follows that even at this early stage in an athlete's career factors which will ultimately affect performance are being formed.

Interaction

Around 2 years of age speech evolves; so too does the ability for the infant to communicate with the world in general. The aspiring individual can talk with others of all ages and communicate likes, dislikes, needs and ideas. Similarly new listening skills develop facilitating the absorption of new ideas, information and knowledge as part of the learning process. It is self-evident that initial levels of understanding are extremely basic and that any communication must be within those parameters. During this period walking becomes more sophisticated and controlled and facilitates the development of running and, as kinaesthesis continues to evolve, judgements that allow for variations in speed. Jumping and landing skills improve, as do related activities such as turning, bending, stretching, pushing and pulling. The individual becomes more aware of her or his body and how it moves and is now able to coordinate movement with intellectual reasoning in play and games, with some degree of confidence. More complex skills that depend upon the integration and coordination of many skills learned individually evolve. These include throwing, catching, punching, patting, kicking and embryonic specific techniques and tactics. These fundamental patterns of movement and perceptual awareness are generally established by the age of 8.

It can be appreciated that if a sport-specific activity, such as kicking a football is taught without a basic understanding of the movement, the need for control of the leg and foot, the direction the limb moves in, the force used and so on, the accuracy of the kick and the distance the ball moves will not be satisfactory. To ensure that a sport-specific technique is taught efficiently and effectively it is essential that the basic movement patterns, not techniques, are learned first.

During this period schools are invaluable in teaching individuals these basic skills in the most general way. Individual and team activities can ensure the development of core actions. Multi-activity or specific sports clubs should identify their aims and objectives at this stage of taking on the role of the school. Teaching and developing general skills not only for the benefit of the individual but for the refinement of techniques latter. Any game or activity should be presented in a very rudimentary manner to facilitate progressive personal development. In most cases sport-specific coaching is out of place.

Co-ordination

From the age of 8 movement patterns can be expanded and refined, mainly because the individual is aware of the position of his or her body or of the 'feel' of a movement, an evolving sense of kinaesthesis. This allows them to modify an action as required. Also, very importantly, the youngster can appreciate intellectually the quality of movement and can understand what is needed. Technical and tactical awareness develop. The skills learned in the previous stages act as foundations for the new and sport-specific ones introduced from now on. This level of development is usually achieved by the age of 12 years. Schools are the ideal vehicle for the development of a wide range of sports skills, and they can offer specific opportunities for those who seek them through clubs and teams. There can be a shift from the general to the specific in the nature of physical activity. Specific sports can be taught, modified to this level of maturation. Sports clubs offer the opportunity for age-related competition and associated levels of preparation. Training regimes and practices used by adults are inappropriate.

Specialisation

From the age of 12 onwards skills and their application develop. There tends to be much more specialisation in specific sports or activities in which the individual is interested. With the onset of puberty about this time and the approach of adulthood there are great changes not only in the physical make-up of the individual but also in behavioural, emotional, sociological and intellectual ways. Other values, relating to family, friends, school and sport begin to be established. By the age of 16 physical and intellectual maturation will be well on the way. Individuals with potential will have been identified through the school/club system and will be able to develop sophisticated techniques and, where appropriate, tactical awareness.

From 16 onwards most individuals who have ability will be involved in specific sports and activities and will be subjected to the progressive training loads and demands of competition, both physical and intellectual. It will be in the later part of this 16–25 period that they will have the degree of maturity to withstand the extremes of the sporting demands that are made of them.

To implement a champion coaching strategy parents, teachers, coaches and others involved in the process have fully to understand the evolutionary process of skill development. They must ensure that they temper their enthusiasm with common sense, and only intervene to modify the natural process if it is appropriate at that level and in a manner that relates to their intellectual and physical development. Trying to rush the process to move on to the next stage without mastery of the present one is a prescription for disaster, a case of trying to run before one can walk!

The sequence of these developmental stages is progressive, in that the skills learned in one phase are the foundation for refinement into more complex ones as they systematically evolve; figure 3.3 identifies the progression. It is very difficult, if not impossible, to teach individual skills or techniques appropriate to development if youngsters have not experienced, let alone mastered, the previous ones. The evolution of these skills seems to follow a progressive pattern. In chronological order these appear to be awareness of:

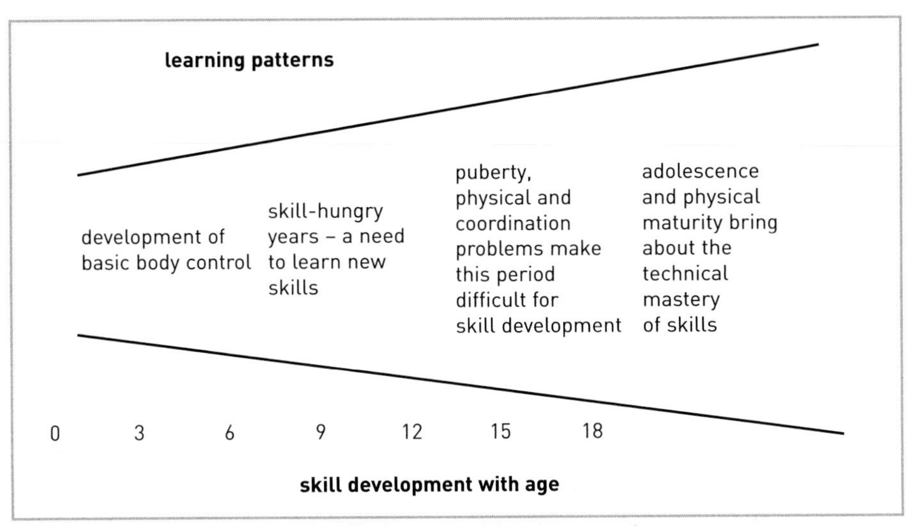

FIG. 3.3 Development of physical skills is sequential and progressive

- being alive
- one's body, limbs, and movement
- one's physical situation and place within the environment
- up, down, left, right and combinations of direction
- time present, future and past
- tempo and rhythm
- co-ordinating limb and whole body movements with vision and other stimuli.

There is also general development of the senses, both individually and combined and integrated:

- vision
- hearing
- touch
- balance
- smell
- taste
- kinaesthesis.

As the maturation process moves on, all these elements can be incorporated into the refinement of slightly more complex skills:

- reaching
- grasping
- sitting
- crawling
- standing
- falling
- walking
- running with variations of pace and style
- jumping with variations in take-off
- landing with variations of feet positions
- rolling
- climbing.

As these movement skills develop there is a need for greater intellectual application. This is particularly the case when selecting the correct movement pattern in response to a given situation, such as:

- pushing
- pulling
- turning
- spinning
- twisting
- bending
- stretching.

Once again, these body movements provide a platform for learning more complex skills that require co-ordination between the whole body and particular parts of it. These skills include:

- throwing
- punching
- patting
- bouncing
- kicking
- catching
- stopping objects with the feet.

Those individuals who seek to develop the talent of athletes have one fundamental problem from the outset. Techniques and tactics used at the very highest levels of sport are those that require physical and intellectual maturity. For this level of attainment it is assumed that individuals also have high levels of strength, speed, endurance and mobility. It has to be accepted that the level of performance is the result of systematic and progressive training over many years. It requires little in the way of insight to realise that youngsters, no matter their developmental stage, do not possess these elements to the same degree as adults.

Those who wish to identify and foster the progression of young athletes have to accept that they cannot teach advanced and complex techniques, let alone their application that requires a high level of maturity, at a stage when the athlete is only just developing elemental skills and co-ordination. Before advanced practices are introduced the foundations of basic movements and their co-ordination have to be established (figure 3.4). Simplistically, a child who cannot throw a ball in a controlled and coordinated fashion is going to have difficulty with a natural progression such as throwing a javelin. To ensure that any sport-specific activity is appropriate it is essential that sports governing bodies produce coaching programmes that reflect the developmental stage of the individual and provide extensive training for those involved.

However, the acquisition and refinement of sporting skill is not quite as straightforward as might be inferred from the process described! The reality is that physical and intellectual development from birth is not constant, it occurs in spurts. Though the developmental phases identified can be associated with periods of infancy, childhood, and adolescence leading into adulthood, not all faculties develop at the same rate.

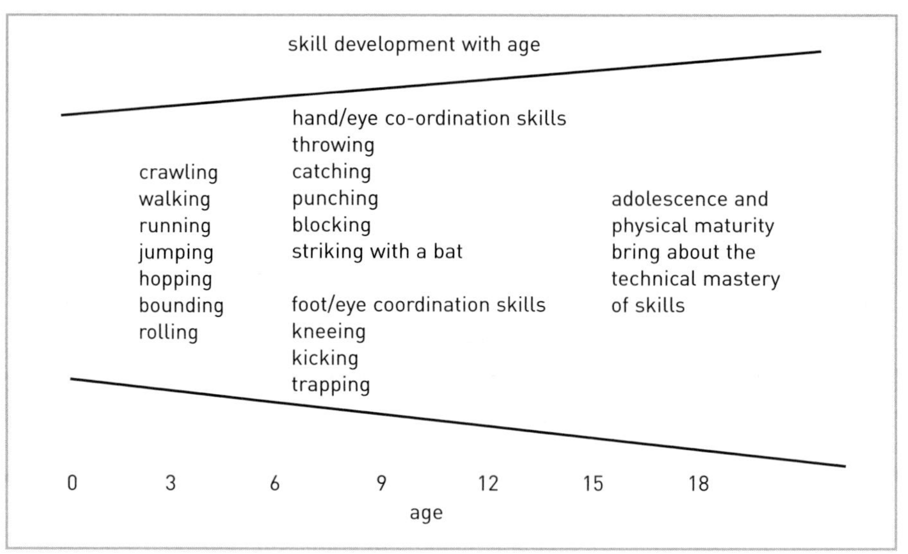

FIG. 3.4 The hierarchy of the skill learning process

PHYSICAL CHANGES

From birth to approximately 8 years the rate of growth for boys and girls is fairly constant. From the age of around 6 the rate of development changes, in particular standing height and limb length begin to increase. This marks the first step on the road to the period in life known as 'puberty' which can be described as the period of change from childhood to adulthood. Recent research has shown that puberty begins much sooner than thought. It can start as early as 6 in girls, and 8 in boys. It can be rapid, dramatic and traumatic as the individual attempts to deal with radical developments in their physical and mental state. This tends to challenge the widely held understanding of puberty as the more striking impact of the second stage, achieved by girls between 10 and 12 years, and boys a little later, between 12 and 14.

The process lasts for five or six years and involves a wide range of changes as hormones pervade the body to coordinate the transformation. Body fat and muscle mass increase and the skeleton grows giving rise to modifications in physique and improvements in strength, reaction time and speed of movement. Cardiovascular and respiratory developments increase endurance. The reproductive organs and secondary sexual characteristics mature.

INTELLECTUAL CHANGES

The physical changes before, during and after puberty are quite obvious. The body of a small child develops into that of an adult. However the hormone-driven changes in the central and peripheral nervous system are not as equally apparent, despite the fact that they are equally dramatic. It has been long held that by late childhood the brain, and associated neural tissue, was fully developed. Recent research in America has found that the brain continues to develop during and after puberty, particulary the prefrontal cortex which is involved in planning, organising, controlling emotions and inhibiting inappropriate behaviour – qualities that seem to be lacking in most teenagers!

It was found that there is a loss of cerebral tissue by the end of the teens. The argument put forward is that the brain becomes more efficient by selectively 'pruning' connections between neurones, destroying the unused and leaving only the well-used ones. The structure of the remaining cells is modified to speed up their transmission of information. As the individual approaches maturity neural connections are fewer but faster. Other research has identified that this pruning process can occur as early as in the womb and shortly after birth and that the second wave of pruning during puberty is due to related hormones triggering this cerebral efficiency drive.

As seen earlier, the brain and nervous system develop in stages. The senses are the first phase, followed by language and lastly executive functions associated with prioritising, organising thoughts and weighing the consequences of actions. They become fully developed at around the age of 25.

CHAPTER 4
SPORT-SPECIFIC TRAINING

It is all very well to identify the physical and mental changes that the developing athlete goes through, but the coach has still to devise a training strategy that will enable the performer to develop sporting skills and competence.

Before attempting to design an appropriate programme for an athlete, several key elements need to be considered. Initially these might include:

- age
- sex
- height
- weight
- present level of performance (how is it assessed?)
- required level of performance (depends on identified goals)
- competition season (and key events)
- facilities and resources available
- time available per day/week
- time of day available to train
- level of commitment.

Though these elements provide a reasonable basis, coaches may well be able to identify additional elements that are relevant to them. It is self-evident that a taller player will have an advantage in basketball, volleyball or high jump, but what are the requirements of a specific sport such as rugby and particular positional demands, and do you know them? The amount of time available for training will markedly affect the rate of progress and the level of performance achieved. Research has shown that the time of day when training occurs may have a marked effect on the rate of improvement.

Facilities too are vital, and the need to be able to get to them is self-evident. An enthusiastic footballer will not be able to play, let alone train, if there is no local club. The availability of a suitable outdoor area, floodlit in winter, an indoor venue or specific equipment, or the lack of these, will affect the development of performance and the continued motivation and enthusiasm of the player.

The most important question that those involved with this process, primarily the athlete, have to address is, what is the the goal for which they are planning? Some might want to participate just for fun and healthy activity, others may aspire to elite performance – everyone has to be honest and realistic.

Any systematic and progressive training programme has to contain four essential components:

Specificity

Training must be specific to the sport and in team games must include particular positional demands. In netball the requirements of goal attack are not the same as goal defence!

Overload

Optimum improvement will only occur if the training is systematic and progressive. Training intensity must subject the individual to levels above normal. As the particular body system improves, so the workload should be commensurately increased.

Adaptation

The associated improvements in performance occur not during the activity itself but during the period afterwards, when the body has recovered. Following activity waste products are removed, energy stores are replenished and tissue is subject to general maintenance and repair. The body adapts to the increased loadings by improving the effectiveness and efficiency of the associated tissue. Sufficient rest must be allowed between training sessions to allow this adaptation to take place. The adaptive processes occur during the recovery phase! The more intense the training the longer the period of recovery required. It is the careful balance between training and recovery that is the key to successful training.

Reversibility

If the training load is insufficient or not progressive or the rest periods are inappropriate performance levels will fall back.

ASSESSMENT

All of those involved in the training process must establish methods of evaluating progress – or lack of it! With swimming and track athletes it is relatively easily done by comparing training or competition times. But, that will not work for football. The number of gaols scored in a game is not a good indicator of the standard of play. Most governing bodies have assessment tests that can be used on a regular basis as part of the general training programme to give some objective evaluation. Evaluating the programme is essential if the coach is to modify it in the light of poor or excellent changes in performance.

The ancient Greeks and Romans understood well the need for systematic training for battle, principles which became readily applicable to gladiators and athletes alike. Further, it has to be acknowledged that over the years experienced coaches in all sports produced successful individuals and teams. They have used tried and tested methods in producing training regimes that work. Though they may not have appreciated the scientific relevance of their thinking, in most cases modern research serves only to confirm that what they thought was the way to go about preparation was founded on current theories of best practice. Too many coaches in the past, and even now, have not been afforded recognition of their efforts and groundbreaking and innovative practices. This lack of respect and recognition of individuals and their expertise has alienated not a few. Their wealth of knowledge has been dismissed by many in their various sports as being old-fashioned and no longer appropriate, a case of throwing the baby out with the bathwater. Sporting success is not a current phenomenon! Experienced coaches or those who work in sports that may not see the application of training theories might be surprised to note how easily current thinking fits established practice. With only scant acknowledgement of recent research they can improve their existing strategies, and with some fine tuning of their programmes achieve marked improvements.

The mechanisms by which the body adapts to strenuous physical activity have only recently begun to be fully understood, as has, similarly, how specific improvements in performance can be achieved by selective activities. In the 1950s

Hans Selye put forward his 'General Adaptation to Stress' theory. He identified the optimum levels of physical and psychological stress or workload which would bring about the maximum adaptation. He identified that if the loadings were excessive or insufficient, then the adaptation process was adversely affected. He further suggested the notion of 'overtraining', both physically and mentally, which occurred as a result of insufficient recovery. His work was developed and put into a more applied sporting context by two, then Eastern Bloc, sports scientists Matveev and Viru. They suggested a cyclical approach to the training/ recovery balance and put forward the concept of the 'periodisation' of training. They observed that the recovery phase more than restored depleted energy levels, it overfilled them; muscle tissue increased in size and strength; the cardiovascular system increased in efficiency; respiratory function increased; associated development of anatomical structures and physiological systems took place, as seen in figure 4.1. This boost in performance was termed 'overcompensation' by Verkohansky, another Eastern Bloc sports scientist. He noted that if the next

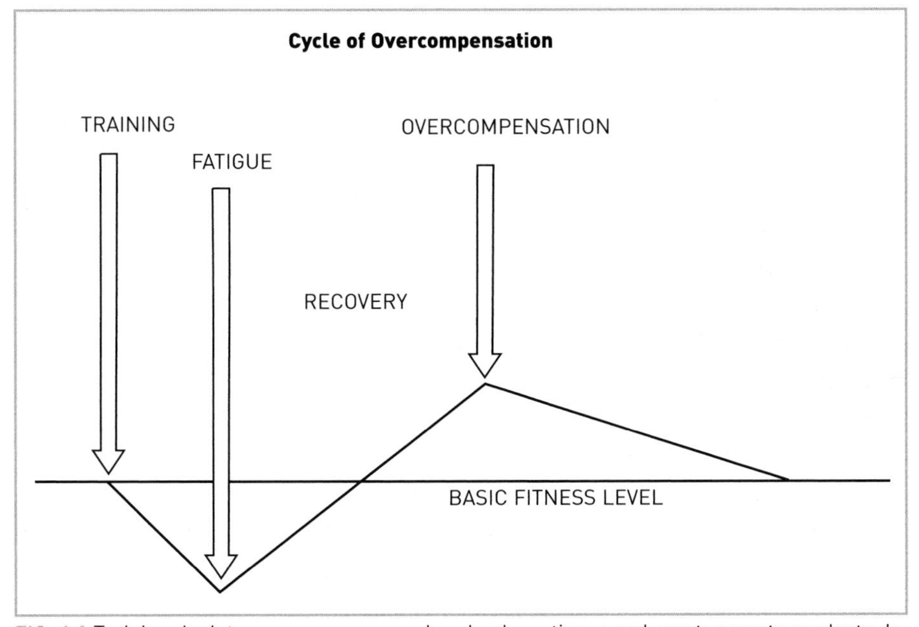

FIG. 4.1 Training depletes energy reserves, breaks down tissue and creates waste products. In the recovery phase, energy stores are overfilled, tissues are repaired and strengthened and waste removal systems improved in preparation for the next period of strenuous activity. If these additional elements are not utilised, body systems will return to their original levels.

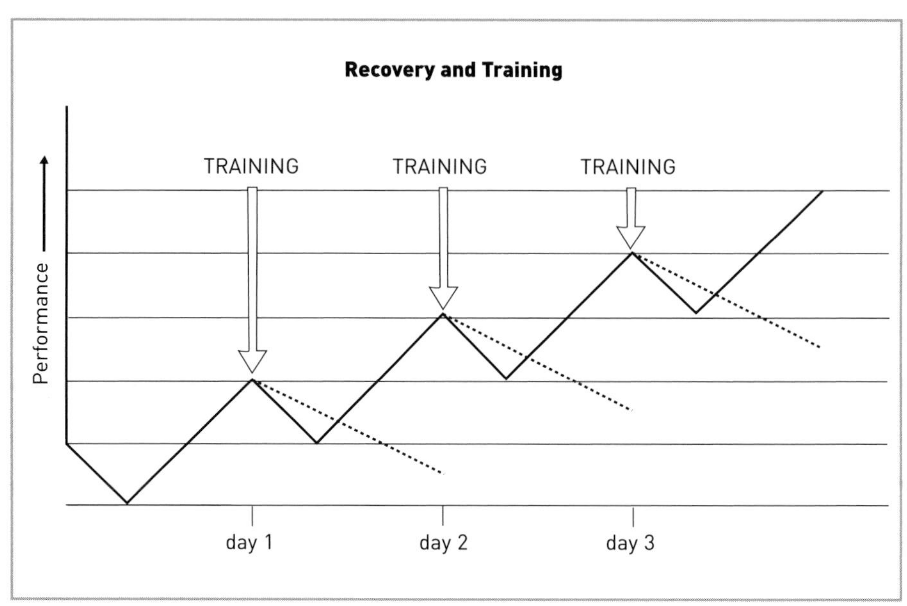

FIG. 4.2 Timing successive periods of training to coincide with the peak of overcompensation optimises the adaptive process.

period of training took place at the right time this overcompensation could be capitalised on (figure 4.2).

It takes time for the effects of a detailed and carefully structured programme of physical activity to appear. Those involved have to make what amount to long-term plans, centred on such things as regular fixtures, important games and specific competitions. Six- or even twelve-week schedules are a little on the short side for planning for a thorough programme to achieve the desired results (figure 4.3); far better are the six-month, one-year, four-year or even longer intervals that occur between the higher levels of advancement. However any period of systematic and progressive preparation that embraces these underpinning principles will have a positive effect on performance. Obviously the longer the period the greater the improvement.

The notion of periodisation of training is not only for the world-class athlete, it is equally – and there is evidence to suggest even more – beneficial for the recreative and novice sportsperson alike. For in the careful design, preparation and implementation of a progressive programme of work any level of talent will be fully utilised and performance levels maximised.

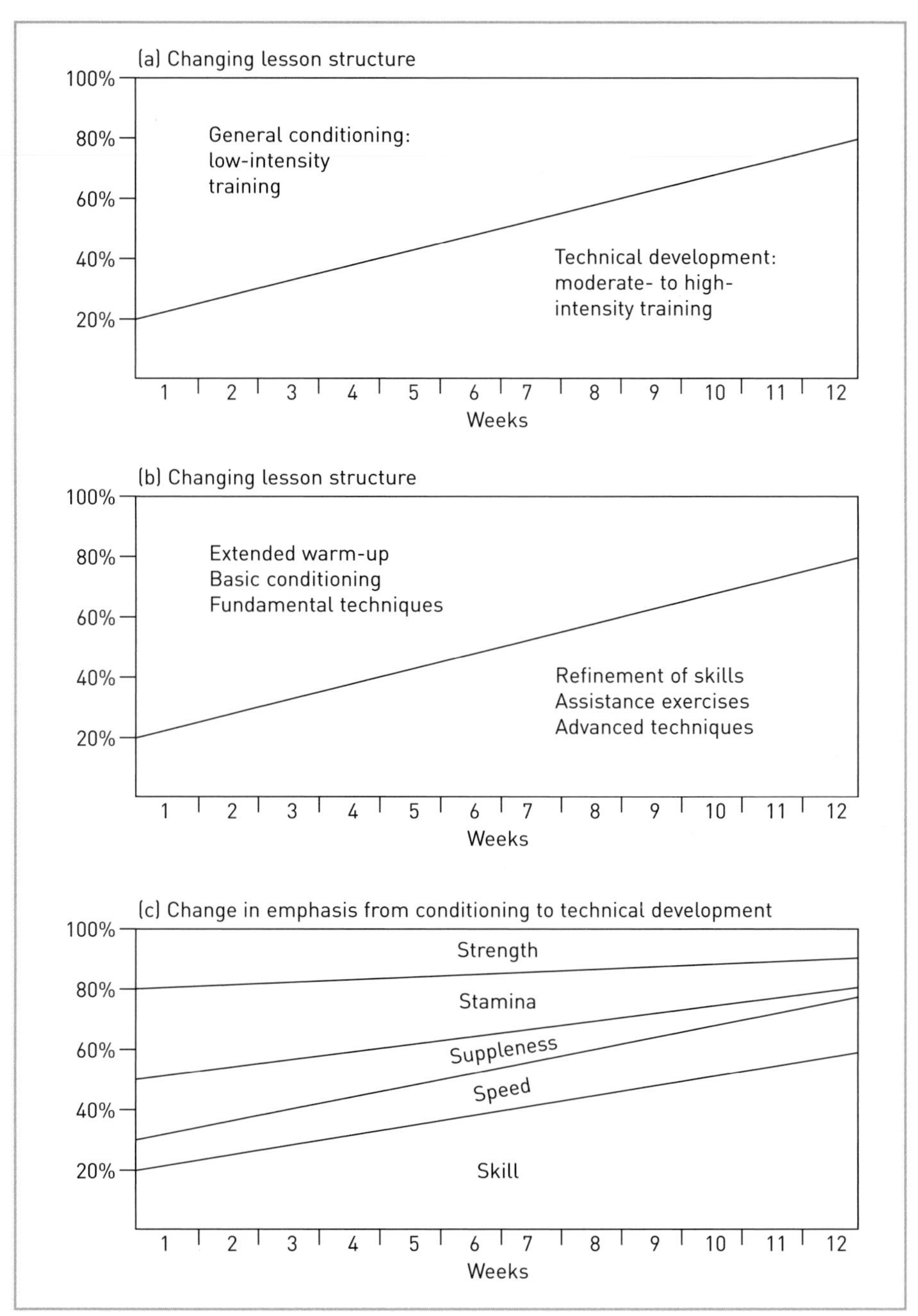

FIG. 4.3 The training emphasis changes from general conditioning to technical refinement over the 12-week period.

PERIODISING TRAINING

Regardless of its duration, preparation time must contain the following four periods:

1 General conditioning
2 Developing basic techniques
3 Special conditioning
4 Establishing advanced techniques.

Though training will involve other aspects it is essential that these must be comprehensively covered. Further it can readily be seen how these components incorporate the adaptive process.

Preparation Phase

The athlete gradually becomes better conditioned to work at the required intensity.

Adaptation Phase

The athlete's skills/technique improve as a result of the training load.

Application Phase

The increased level of sport-specific fitness enables the development of skills/ technique to meet the higher expectations in performance/competence.

Recovery Phase

The body recovers from heavy training through a period of active rest in which the activity or the training emphasis changes. Essentially the body systems that have been subjected to specific overload are allowed a period of recuperation while others are temporarily targeted. For example after a period of particularly intense football training, for a short time the squad might keep active by playing basketball, rugby or squash, as the coach feels appropriate.

DESIGNING THE PROGRAMME

The examples presented in this section embody all these elements. Simplistically there is a move from light general activity to intensive specific application as the schedule unfolds. The emphasis in training moves through a highly specific time line. As will be developed later, the phases of emphasis are crucial in enabling improvements in performance and avoiding injury.

The sequence of emphasis is:

1 Strength
2 Stamina
3 Suppleness
4 Speed
5 Skill
6 (p)Sychology

Each period of focused effort serves as a platform for the next, in a progressive manner. Interestingly if the participation of an athlete, by choice or injury, suddenly stops then the principle of reversibility comes into operation and fitness is lost in the reverse order to which it was developed. That is:

First:	(p)Sychology – competition/performance motivation
Second:	Skill – absolute technical excellence
Third:	Speed – precise timing/reaction time/speed of movement
Fourth:	Suppleness – extreme range of movement
Fifth:	Stamina – anaerobic precedes aerobic deterioration
Sixth:	Strength – sport-specific precedes general deterioration

Figure 4.3 shows an example of how the coordination, balance of training and emphasis on specific elements would change in a 12-week training programme. In the case of holidays or training breaks the percentage loss of a specific element will depend upon the length of time off. The wily coach will be able to modify the programme to address the shortcomings speedily.

No matter how training is manipulated to achieve the desired result, the underpinning element is the cycle of training and supercompensation. The critical feature of this process is the period of recovery when all the systems that have been overloaded can fully recover and adapt. For most athletes, training every other day – that is, three or four times a week – is ideal, since it allows for a day's rest in between, enabling the individual to be fully recovered for the next session. Generally, the fitter the athlete the faster the recovery. An elite performer might be able to train every day because she or he recuperates at an accelerated rate. It is vital that the coach ensures that athletes have fully recovered from previous sessions before commencing another!

It can be seen in figure 4.1 that the best time to train is during the period of overcompensation from the previous session when energy levels have been more than topped up, and body systems have been subject to repair and their functions enhanced. The ability to train at these specific times is the key to the increased rate of progress and overall standard of performance. For the elite performer who needs to train most days at least once, the coach can manipulate the type, intensity, and volume of work to enable full recovery between sessions. Figure 4.4 shows how a coach can construct such a progressive weekly schedule. Each week's programme has to fit into a much longer period in a systematic manner that ensures week on week and, most certainly by the end, overall improvement.

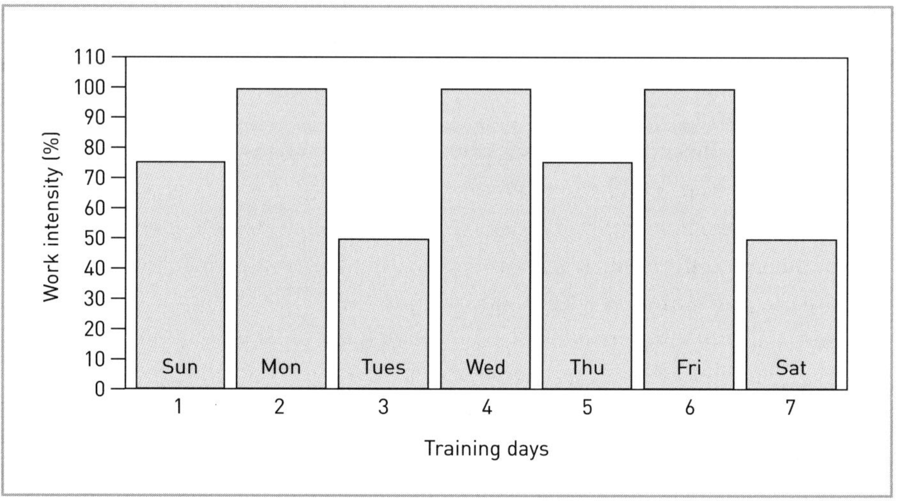

FIG. 4.4 The training load can be varied through the week by balancing intensive training with less demanding sessions.

Periodisation can be split into component parts. Coaches can be heard using jargon: here are some examples, which we will return to later:

Microcycle: In a short programme this might be one day's training; in a longer one possibly a week.

Mesocyle: In a short programme this might be one week's training; in a longer one anywhere between one month and five!

Macrocyle: In a short programme the whole envisaged period of training/preparation or competition might be twelve weeks; in a longer one, six months or a year.

For an elite performer who is aspiring to Olympic success the definitions might be: microcycle – one month; mesocycle – one year; macrocycle – four years.

The former Eastern Bloc would plan training for children not just for one four-year cycle, i.e. for the next Olympics, but for eight years (the Olympics after next), and in some cases for twelve years (the one after that). Micro-, meso- and macrocycles of mere mortals and their permutations pale into insignificance in the presence of such Olympians. The complexities of such preparations necessitated the development of sophisticated computer programmes. Incidently, the painstaking preparations and attention to detail produced an unnervingly high success rate. In designing an appropriate training programme the coach of St Chad's under-11 football team should have no fear!

As the weeks of any programme progress the volume and quantity of work in a microcyle and mesocycle are manipulated to achieve the desired result. Figure 4.3 shows how there is a shift in emphasis of the actual content of sessions from the more general to the specific. During the early stages emphasis is on extended warm-up and basic conditioning. Assuming that two or three techniques or drills are introduced each week, as the schedule develops more and more time is spent revising the previous week's skills and teaching new ones. There is obviously less and less time for basic conditioning, though some will always be included in every session. Towards the latter stages of the macrocycles the constant repetition of skills itself produces specific conditioning and encourages the honing of that fine edge of excellence.

For the 'hands-on' practical coach the mechanisms of periodisation might seem inappropriate or even a waste of time. But even the most cynical coach might recognise:

The preparation period (off-season): This phase in training is characterised by the maintenance and development of the fitness needed to train hard.

The pre-competition period (pre-season): During this phase there is a marked shift from quantity to quality. Skill development and performance become central to the work.

The competition period (season): As the time for high-level performance arrives the focus of training is on high-intensity activity. The very specific demands of competition or playing, both physical and psychological, are well rehearsed.

Figure 4.5 should reassure coaches that many of their established practices are reflected in current thinking. They got most, if not all, of it right after all. But no coach is complacent; there is a constant search to improve training programmes to keep one step ahead of the opposition. Training theory can offer an opportunity for critically evaluating preparation for improved performance.

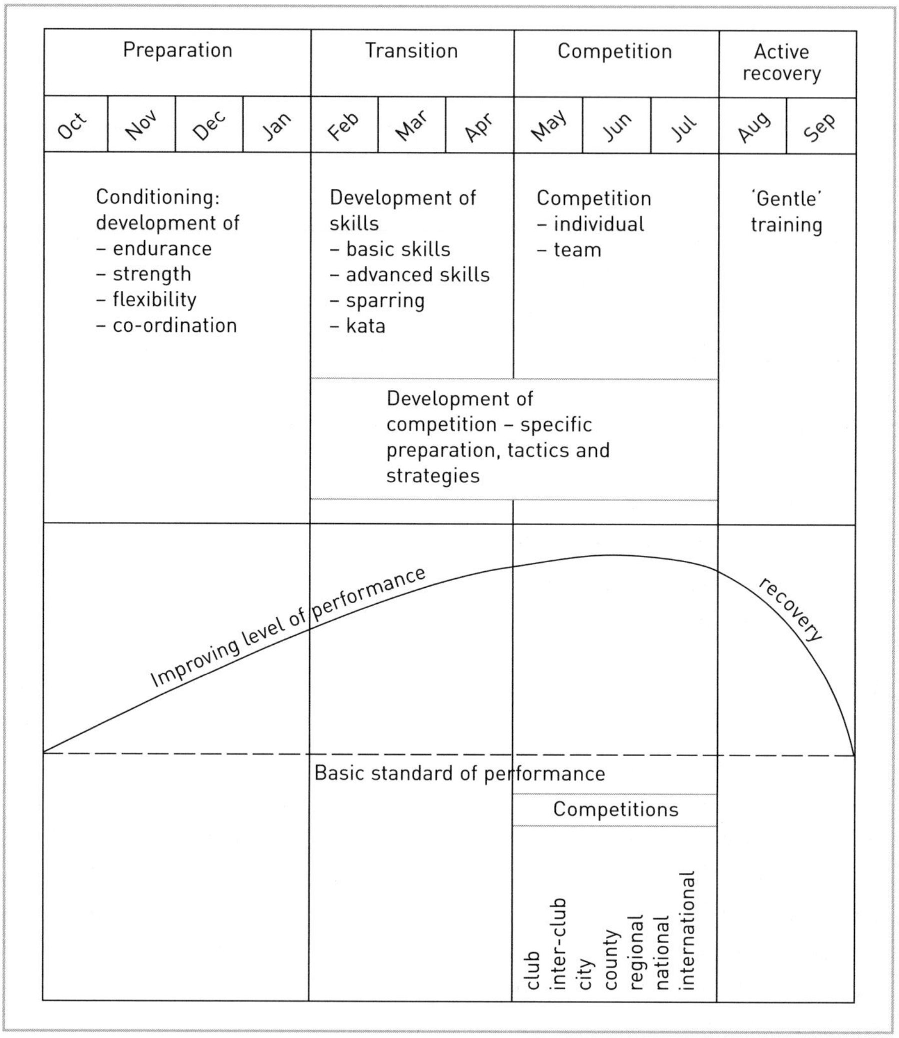

Preparation	Transition	Competition	Active recovery
Oct, Nov, Dec, Jan	Feb, Mar, Apr	May, Jun, Jul	Aug, Sep
Conditioning: development of - endurance - strength - flexibility - co-ordination	Development of skills - basic skills - advanced skills - sparring - kata	Competition - individual - team	'Gentle' training
	Development of competition - specific preparation, tactics and strategies		

Improving level of performance

recovery

Basic standard of performance

Competitions

club
inter-club
city
county
regional
national
international

FIG. 4.5 The training and competition year for a karate student. The main competition period in this example is in the summer months. The general principles are similar for other summer-based competitive sports such as athletics, tennis and cricket.

CHAPTER 5
FITNESS AND CONDITIONING

Coaching champions is not an easy challenge for those concerned. Simplistically, the level of sporting excellence is the criterion that marks out the elite. But success in any competitive situation is the tip of the iceberg; it gives no regard to the hours, weeks and years of training that have produced the triumphant moment in time. Great accolades are given to the athletes, but all too often the knowledge, understanding and commitment of the coach is given scant regard.

For success in any sport the coach has to identify key elements:

- the physical and psychological demands of the sport and any specific positional requirements
- the systematic training requirements that facilitate progressive levels of performance.

With these variables in mind the coach must balance the training requirements to meet the needs of the competitive environment and enable success for the athlete or team. Though to a greater or lesser degree all sports have common physical demands, in most cases the specific requirements of each will be quite different. In the adaptive processes of training particular requirements of a sport are highlighted by the emphasis placed on them in preparation. The coach has to identify the particular aspects of fitness that s/he wants to develop. Figure 5.1 is an example of an assessment sheet to help identify the specific elements that are required for a sport or a position. (If the elements shown are not relevant to a specific activity it should be quite easy to create a check sheet that is.)

As sport science has developed over recent years what was once a reasonably simple situation has become very complex and confusing. As research has

Sport/ Position	Speed	Reaction time	Mobility	Flexibility	Agility	Maximum strength	Relative strength	Explosive strength	Aerobic endurance	Anaerobic endurance	Speed endurance	Local muscular endurance	Skill
													10
Training variables													
Training													
Grading													
Competition													
Age													
Gender													
Ability													

FIG. 5.1 Give a score out of 10 for each of the various components of fitness identified. The scoring can relate to a game such as football or to a specific position such as goalkeeper or centre forward. The scores can be noted for different aspects of preparation such as general training, grading in the martial arts, competition and any other factor such as age, gender and ability.

progressed the physical and psychological aspects of sport have been analysed to the nth degree. For example, classical medicine identified one type of skeletal muscle. Then relatively recently it was suggested that there are two types of skeletal muscle fibre, which helped explain an individual's excellence in endurance or speed activities. Then, to account for the effect of training, there were three. When it was realised that a mere three types of fibre did not explain the subtle differences manifest in different sports, even more were proposed. Then it was suggested that there really was only one type of skeletal muscle fibre, and that it adapted to the type of work to which it was subjected.

Because of the confusing multitude of theories, terminologies and current 'in' ideas perhaps a more classical approach to the definition of these components of fitness is appropriate. Not only will this enable the coach to identify the elements which are prerequisite in a sport but it will give a process upon which present theories can be superimposed. For many years coaches, teachers and athletes have broken down sports fitness in a simple mnemonic, the 'S' factors (as above, in chapter 4).

- Speed
- Strength
- Suppleness
- Stamina
- Skill
- (p)Sychology

Each sport or position within a team game will have its own blend of these elements. Soccer will differ from swimming. A rugby forward will have specific needs compared to the fullback. When evaluating the balance of the 'S' factors in the training of athletes the coach has to assess the particular importance each one has in excellent performance.

ANALYSING THE 'S' FACTORS

Speed

The increase in speed is by and large one of the major precepts of training. It is a complex quality that has two main aspects:

- moving a single limb at speed as in a throw, punch or kick
- moving the entire body at speed.

Movement at speed is a sophisticated refinement of technique and as such is part of the total maturational process (figure 5.2). Technical excellence must be acquired at slower speeds before any accelerated movement is performed. Connective tissue and associated systems that produce a specific pattern of movement must be allowed to adapt to the stresses of particular loading before moving on to the next. Any attempt to move connective tissue and associated systems at speed before they have adapted to the forces applied is a recipe for disaster. If muscles, joints, limbs or the whole body are moved at speed before they have been conditioned to do so or in an incorrect pattern of movement, or with poor technique, injury will result.

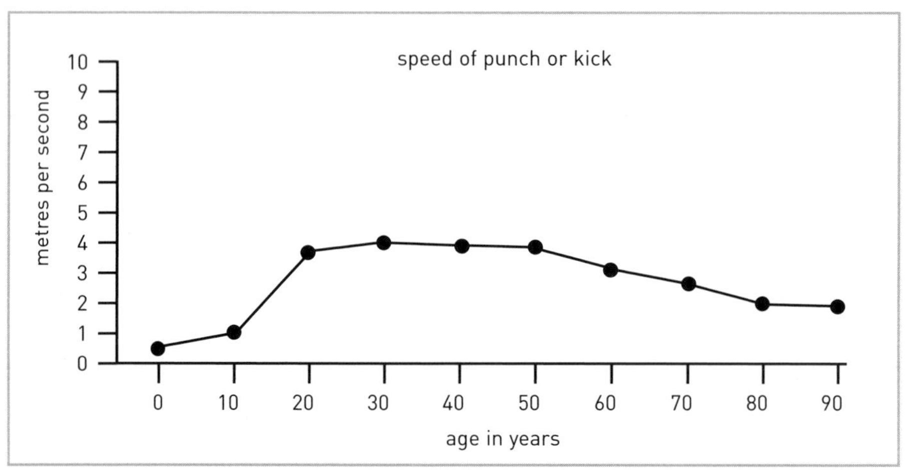

FIG. 5.2 Speed of movement improves dramatically after puberty and levels off in the mid 20s.

In many sports the term 'speed' is used to refer to reaction time, the ability to respond to specific cues from the external environment or within the body itself. This a complex quality derived from a range of interrelated elements.

- **Perception time**: how long it takes to be aware that something is happening. This usually involves the senses of sight, sound and touch detecting the source of an event.
- **Processing time**: how long it takes to identify the nature of the activity; for instance, in football, that there is a pass coming towards you, not a tackle, and at what angle, speed and height it will arrive. In cricket, what kind of delivery the batsman must face.
- **Selection time**: having identified the nature of the activity, the appropriate skill or technique has to be decided.
- **Movement time**: having selected the appropriate technique it must be assessed how long it will take to perform it.

Each one of these aspects may only take a fraction of a second but in their integrated form give rise to an overall reaction time. The coach must devise training practices that will reduce the time it takes to process each stage. Any difficulty in a particular element will markedly affect overall reaction time. For example, a deterioration in eyesight will affect the time it takes to identify the cue and what is happening accurately. If the athlete should wrongly guess, misinterpret a cue, select an incorrect response, or move too slowly it will result in a poor reaction time. Developing reaction time or any of its components can only take place over a period of time.

Strength

Just as with speed, the concept of the quality of strength is varied and complicated. What are the similarities in the strength requirements of a 100m sprinter, a rugby scrum-half, a gymnast or a shot putter? Each has strength requirements in its own specific way. Perhaps a definition of strength or types of strength might be helpful. The physiologist's definition of strength is 'the tension or force that a muscle or group of muscles can exert against a resistance'. This merely points out the self-evident fact that when muscles contract they produce a force. Strength levels increase naturally with age particularly following puberty (figure 5.3). However hormonal differences between the sexes can influence the effect of strength training (figure 5.4).

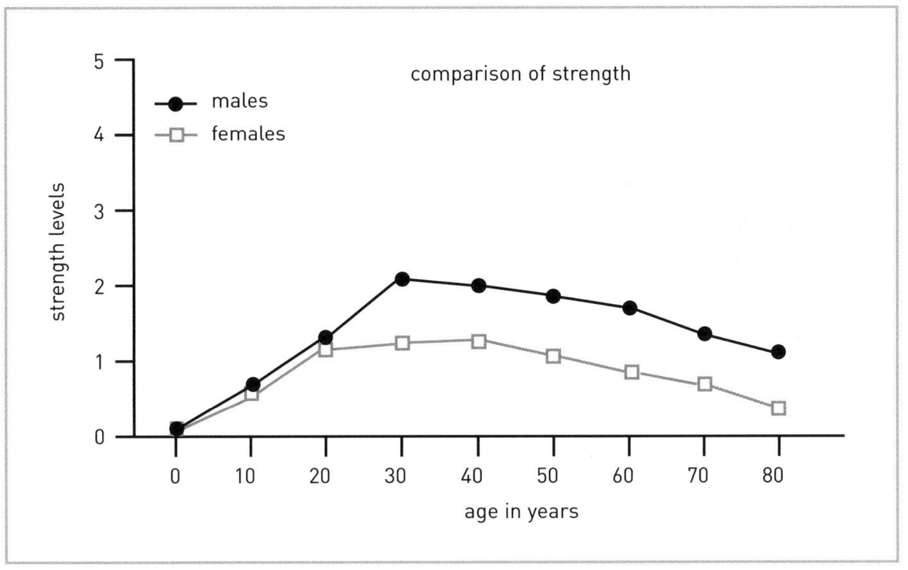

FIG. 5.3 For both sexes, following puberty there is a rapid increase in strength levels, which peak in the mid to late 20s.

A further maturational element that influences the development of strength and is integral with speed is the differentiation of muscle fibres. Broadly speaking

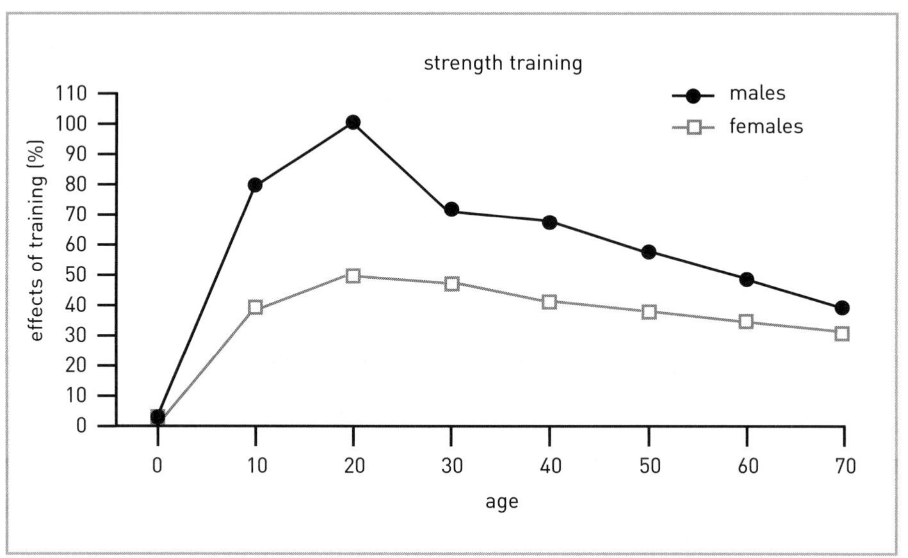

FIG. 5.4 The influence of hormonal changes during and after puberty markedly affect the manner in which males and females respond to strength training.

before puberty muscle tissue is homogenous but afterwards forms two distinct types:

- Fast-twitch fibres: these produce speed of contraction and work of high intensity, but only for short periods – used in sprinting, jumping, throwing and all power activities.
- Slow-twitch fibres: these enable sustained work but at relatively low levels of intensity – used in distance running, repetition of patterns of movement and all endurance activities.

Fibre differentiation occurs around and following puberty and will influence all training and competitions that require these distinct qualities (figure 5.5).

Maximum Strength

'The greatest tension or force which the neuro-muscular system is capable of generating in one conscious effort.' The coach has to determine if it is the requirement of the sport to perform a single technique just once with maximum effort. Whereas it is self-evident in weightlifting, what of squash?

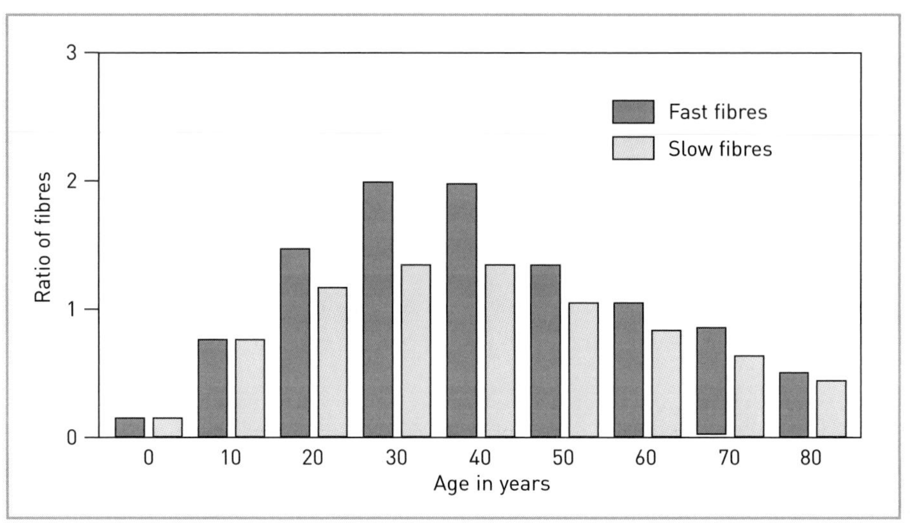

FIG. 5.5 Fast-twitch fibres, which enable speed of movement, develop quickly after puberty and peak in the mid 20s. The number of these fibres declines in later years, but slow-twitch fibres remain in large numbers.

Relative Strength

'The greatest tension or force that the neuromuscular system can exert as a proportion of bodyweight.' This type of strength has been referred to as the power-to-weight ratio. It is not the total force produced or the weight lifted that is critical, but how it relates to the athlete's bodyweight. Lin weighs 50 kilos and can squat 100 kilos, Carole weighs 75 kilos and can also squat 100 kilos. Both netballers can squat with the same load, but Lin has managed twice her bodyweight, whereas Carole has not. Therefore in proportion to bodyweight, Lin is the stronger. Many sports require athletes to move their own bodyweight, as in basketball, football and high-jump, as opposed to an external load, as in throwing the discus. Gymnastics is a classic example of this type of strength.

Explosive Strength

'The ability of the muscles to contract and generate force explosively.' The development of technique is generally the main focus of training, followed closely by the facility to perform skills at speed with a gradation of force up to maximum levels. Power is the capacity of muscles to generate optimum force in the shortest possible time. Due to the short contraction period, muscles may not be able to develop their potential maximum strength. Is the development of maximum strength important in either of these situations?

Speed Endurance

'The ability of muscles to continue working at maximal effort in an environment of the ever-increasing presence of fatigue products.' Any athlete working at speed even for a relatively short period of time will experience a rapid build-up of fatigue products, such as lactic acid (a 400 metres runner is a classic example). If the sport requires participants to be able to function in such conditions, training must reflect this.

Strength Endurance

'The ability of muscles to generate maximal force effort in an environment of the ever-increasing presence of fatigue products.' As with speed endurance, it might be important for the sport that the participant can generate maximum force for a long period, as with a sustained push by the forwards in a rugby scrum or a sustained pull in a tug of war.

Local Muscular Endurance

'The ability of muscles to generate force in an environment of the ever-increasing presence of products at a local level.' If a middle distance athlete runs for a sustained period, by and large only the leg muscles will become tired. However the muscles of the trunk and arms, which are not working anywhere near as intensively, could continue working long after the legs are totally fatigued. If strength training is directed towards the legs the onset of waste products affecting performance during a race will be delayed. It is for the coach to identify specific muscle groups that enhance performance or might be the weak links, and isolate and develop them by means of specific exercises or training methods.

Suppleness

As with other 'S' factors the coach must have a clear understanding of the precise requirements of the activity. Suppleness is used as a catch-all term that embraces different qualities and is used to cover any or all of the following definitions.

Range of Movement

'The angle through which a limb or part of the body can move with respect to specific joint or series of joints.' If the coach wants a high-hurdler to develop hip mobility to facilitate improvements in lead and trail leg technique, exercises that isolate the joints involved need to be introduced. A hurdler could be very flexible in the pelvic region but have poor range of movement in the wrist. Any individual is not equally flexible in every joint, some will be better than others. There is no such thing as a flexible or inflexible athlete. The coach has to establish the specific joints that need isolating and create the appropriate improvement strategies. One of the advantages the young athlete has is natural mobility. This faculty begins to tail off somewhere between 16 and 18 years (figure 5.6). However, it is very easy to develop a range of movement that can lead to joint instability and articular problems later in life. Coaches should take care with any extreme movements or joint isolation exercises

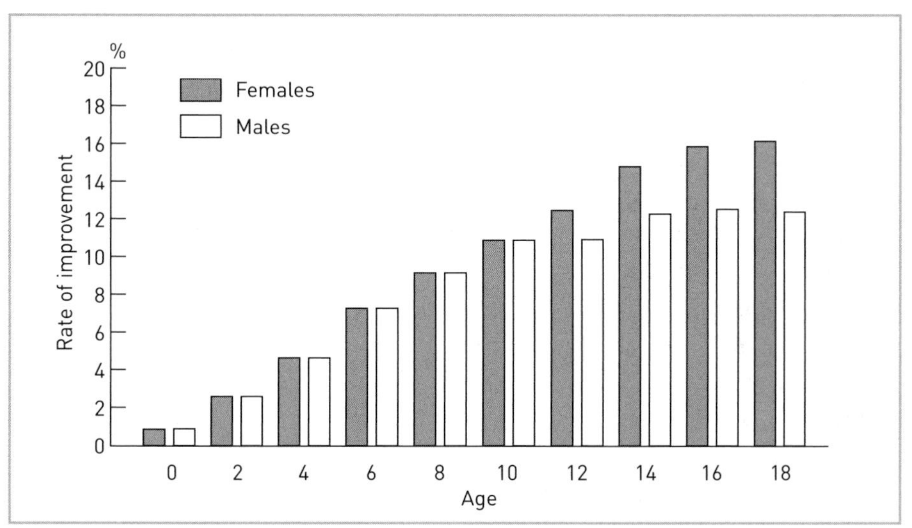

FIG. 5.6 Young athletes are very mobile in all joints. Following puberty, girls have an advantage over boys, but by 18 natural mobility is in decline.

Mobility

'The maximum range of movement that is attainable in a joint or series of joints by means of a conscious sustained effort.' Just because a joint has the potential to move through a wide range does not mean the player can fully utilise it. Unless muscle groups that facilitate the movement required are specifically developed to work in these extreme ranges the possibilities will not be exploited. In such situations injury is a distinct possibility.

Flexibility

'The absolute range of movement that is attainable in a joint or series of joints in a momentary effort, with the help of equipment or a partner.' The range of movement that can be achieved, such as rotating the hip in a hurdling motion while in a standing position, is markedly different to that obtained in a 'hurdle sit' position on the floor or the limb being 'assisted' through the required range by a partner.

Agility

'The range of movement in a series of joints that enables the whole body in one coordinated action to perform complex movements.' Many techniques require that various parts of the body move at the same time in an integrated manner, in different directions and often at speed, to produce excellence. An example would be a full twisting double back somersault in a gymnastics floor exercise. If the athlete is expected to move as an integrated system of flexible sub-units this must be reflected in the preparation.

Suppleness will not develop without highly specific training, and the overload principle is applicable in any planning. Technique will be negatively affected by poor suppleness; as it improves, so will the quality of movement. As a range of movement is achieved the joint must be put under slightly more stress to achieve even more. And when this range has been consolidated the cycle repeats itself.

Stamina

Endurance in some form or another is an essential aspect of all sport. The very training environment itself is based upon the individual's ability to work for relatively long periods of time, often quite intensively. Traditionally training sessions last between one and two hours, athletes have to develop a suitable level of stamina to participate fully and obtain the maximum benefit. However, during the session the participants will not work one sustained level but will be involved in bouts of low and high intensity, with periods of rest, lighter work or active recovery. To meet the demands of training and competition energy is provided through two systems.

The Aerobic System

'In the presence of oxygen, the ability of the muscle and associated tissue to work for sustained periods.' This process ensures a constant supply of energy for a sustained period but at a relatively low level of intensity. Athletes may be required in training to work for over an hour but if they are the intensity of work will be low. Aerobic work is characterised when sufficient oxygen is available for active tissue to meet its demand (figure 5.7). It is sometimes called the 'steady state' theory, where energy demand is matched by oxygen supply. Aerobic work has several advantages. Muscular work in the presence of oxygen predominantly produces carbon dioxide and water as waste products. This material has to be removed as quickly as possible or their build-up will interfere with the working muscles. The body's aerobic systems are very efficient at moving these particular products and providing extra fuel for energy production, but these are dependent on an efficient transport system, which is dependent upon:

- the efficiency of the heart to beat faster as a muscular pump to increase blood flow
- the ability of blood vessels to transport blood efficiently to and through active tissue, bringing nutrients and oxygen and removing waste products

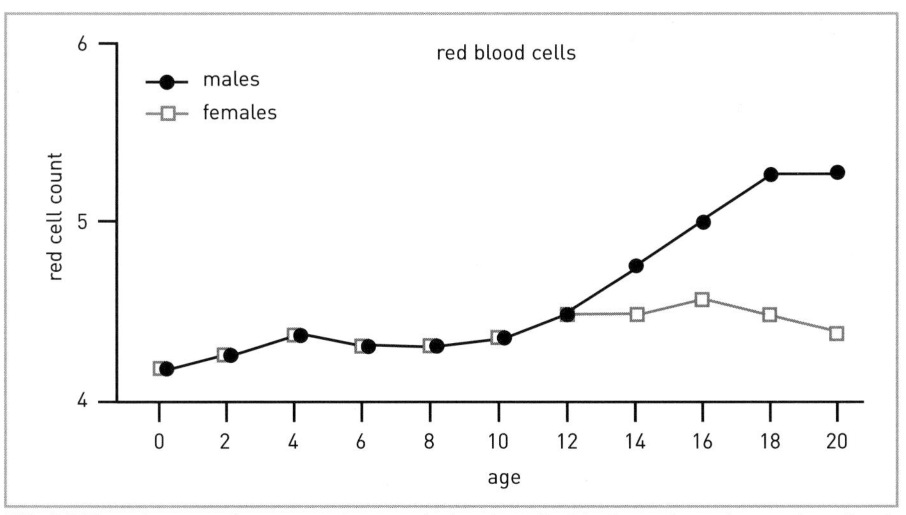

FIG. 5.7 The transport of oxygen and removal of carbon dioxide depends on the number of red blood cells. Both sexes have similar counts until after puberty, when boys have more.

- the efficiency of the lungs to work faster to assimilate oxygen from the atmosphere and transport it to circulating blood while at the same time removing carbon dioxide in a reverse process
- the capacity of the blood to carry gases and nutrients.

Aerobic work is characterised by the integration of the heart, lungs and circulating blood to match the energy demand. The adaptation of these systems to the work rate not only increases their efficiency and capacity to work at even higher levels as the cyclical process continues, but also has valuable health benefits (figure 5.8). The coach must identify strategies to develop long periods of low intensity work if the sport or training require it.

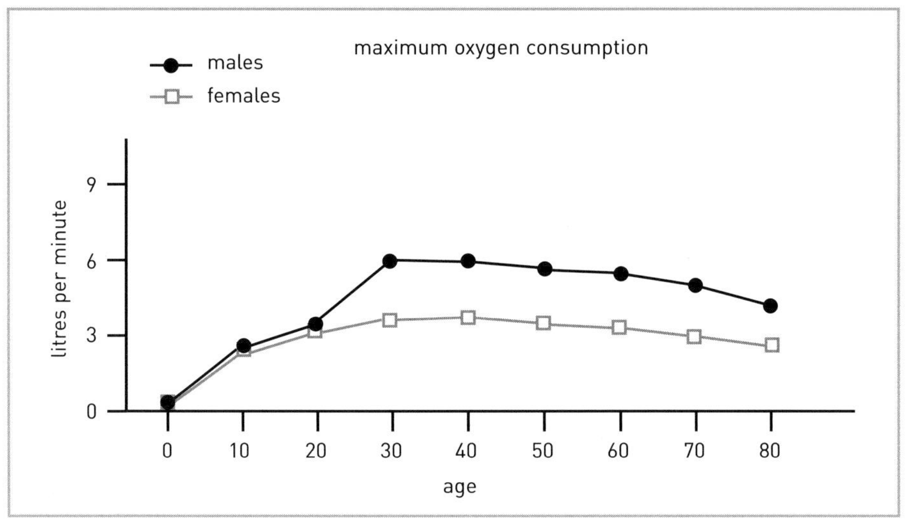

FIG. 5.8 The maximum amount of oxygen that the body can utilise per minute directly affects the amount of work that can be done.The more oxygen, the greater the quantity and quality of work.

The Anaerobic System

'The ability of the muscles and associated tissues to work intensively without oxygen.' Most training activities and sports, particularly team games, require short bursts of intense effort. Muscle work is at such a high rate that oxygen cannot be transported fast enough to satisfy the demand. One of the qualities of muscle is that it can work maximally for short periods without oxygen, but there is a price to pay! When muscles work anaerobically lactic acid is produced as a waste product. This material is viscous and not easily removed. As intensive work continues, lactic acid levels build up in the muscles to a point that they markedly reduce energy output. The build-up of lactic acid is associated with minor swelling, localised stiffness and pain after intense periods of activity. If the athlete has to work anaerobically in his or her sport or training the coach has to identify the intensity of loadings appropriate to individual fitness levels. The adaptive processes that facilitate the adaptation of aerobic systems are different to anerobic ones, and training must reflect these differences.

The situation is exacerbated by the fact that, though different, both systems can and do operate in a coordinated manner. Aerobic work is characterised by an efficient transport system, which is helpful in resolving the problem of the build-up of lactic acid during anaerobic activity. This process is useful during periods of activity and in the following rest and subsequent recovery. Anaerobic athletes need a component of aerobic work in their training to facilitate this process:

- to speed up the removal of waste products, especially lactic acid
- to bring large amounts of oxygen to break down remaining lactic acid into a more readily disposable product and at the same time recycling some of it as fuel.

The efficiency of the transport system will not only enable the athlete to recover faster but also to repeat the action again more quickly. Most sports require periods of intense and light work that is facilitated by the integration of the two systems.

Energy Systems

Just as there is a difference between aerobic and anaerobic work within each system there are subtleties that the coach must consider. Within the anaerobic system specific subdivisions will meet particular energy demands. The biochemistry of these systems is complex and their actual duration less than precise, depending on which theory is currently in fashion, but the following guidelines will serve to aid the coach in her or his assessment of the sport and the needs of training.

Anaerobic activity:

- immediate – less than a second, e.g. weightlifting, and within a game, such as a rugby penalty kick
- short term – up to five seconds, e.g. a gymnastics vault, and within a game, such as a hockey sprint from attack to defend
- medium term – up to 15 seconds, e.g. the 110 metres hurdles for men, and within a game, such as a short rally in badminton
- long term – up to 60 seconds, e.g. the 100 metres freestyle, and within a game, such as a sustained attack in soccer.

Integrated aerobic and anaerobic activity: for periods of intensive work longer than 60 seconds the anaerobic and aerobic systems work in a coordinated manner:

- up to three minutes – e.g. running 800 metres
- up to five minutes – e.g. 400 metres freestyle.

Aerobic activity:

- long-duration, relatively low-intensity work – lasts as long as required, e.g. a marathon.

The coach has a problem. First the specific energy demands of a sport have to be evaluated. This is fairly easy with some sports, for example athletics, where seemingly an energy system matches a distance, and running the marathon, which is aerobic work. A game such as football is more complex because it lasts 90 minutes, which is aerobic; but that time is made up of numerous periods of immediate, short-, medium- and long-term bouts of intensive anaerobic activity. In a game situation the different demands of a position have to be analysed, and a training programme that mirrors them has to be devised. The training of a goalkeeper is totally different to that of a fullback or a forward. There is no such thing as team training where every player does the same thing.

This analysis of the different energy systems has to made if a player or team is to be successful. As previously pointed out, the body adapts to the work it is subjected to. This principle applies equally to energy systems: they will adapt to the precise loadings they are subjected to. For example, shuttle runs will develop the short-term anaerobic systems and no other. Long aerobic runs will not improve the immediate anaerobic production of energy, though they may aid the rate of recovery. If training is to be successful it has to be specific not only to the technical demands of the sport but to the specific energy systems required.

Skill

The development of sporting skills is the result of many years' practice and preparation. All too often a youngster displays an aptitude for a particular sport, which is taken to mean that he or she will automatically develop to the highest levels. An ability to perform techniques which mimic those required of an elite performer is not the same as being able actually to perform those actions. For example a youngster who seems to have an 'innate' ability, a 'natural' in high jumping, and can manage a height of 1.50m cannot actually jump over 2.4m, which is what elite performers do! Because of their age they do not have the physical or mental maturity. I have yet to see an extremely talented 8-year-old turning out for the national side or a 10-year-old marathon world record holder.

I am reminded of a situation that occurred – and still might do – in Karate. A female joined a club and very quickly was challenging for the national championships in Kata, a predetermined series of techniques linked together in a formal structure. Her innate ability and natural aptitude for the sport was noted. The problem arose when she was asked to show her skills in Kumite, competition fighting. The results were disastrous. It was then discovered that the Karateka had an extensive background in dance and could quickly master the choreography and detail of the movements of karate techniques like any dance sequence. But being able to perform the movements as a dance as opposed to using them in a competitive environment is not the same thing. Looking good is not the same as being good. And because of the trauma of growth, particulary puberty, there is little relationship to levels of performance early and late in the process. A good 'young 'un' may not be a good 'old 'un' and, unfortunately, very rarely is.

The development of any skill is a physical manifestation of a great many internal physiological processes in the athlete's neuromuscular system. The coach has to understand that outward appearances can be deceptive! It could well be that on the two or three occasions when a technique was performed well it was more down to good luck than design! And the fact that a player was less than competent on two or three attempts at a particular skill, must not be taken to mean that in the main performance is unsound. Occasional observation by any onlooker may not fully reflect the actuality. The learning of skills does not happen at a constant rate. Most coaches will have noticed that there appears to be an initial period of rapid improvement that very soon tapers off. At this levelling-off point many athletes become bored and motivation to continue to practise a technique or drill drops. This is a critical point in skill learning if the technique is to be ingrained.

Sport skills are learned through a recognised sequence of stages:

Stage 1: A rudimentary attempt hardly recognisable as a specific action. The athlete is introduced to a skill or drill and has the key coaching points identified by demonstration and instruction and fully understands the specific pattern of movement. By 'having a go' the individual will begin to 'feel' the action and how to perform it. It is very much a trial and error process but with supportive feedback from the coach and a modicum of luck some of the better efforts might have a vague resemblance to what is wanted.

Stage 2: A crude but recognisable effort. With practice the player becomes able to reproduce a crude but readily identifiable attempt at the technique. The overall quality of skill may be poor but it can be reproduced as and when necessary. Once again support and help from the coach is essential.

Stage 3: Technical refinement. By repeating the technique under careful supervision with a flow of feedback the athlete is able gradually to correct errors and develop technical excellence.

Stage 4: Technical adaptation. With continued repetition of excellent technique the neuromuscular systems involved in a movement physically adapt to the pattern of movement. The technique becomes ingrained. Every time the technique is performed the response will be automatic. The input of the coach is vital in this process since it is essential that correct technique is established. Too often bad technique is a result of lack of feedback throughout the process resulting in the athlete building in an incorrect movement pattern. The coach has to accept responsibility for that! It is the coach who plans, implements and manages the learning process!

Stage 5: Physiological adaptation. With continued practice over a long period of time not only do the neuromuscular systems adapt to ingrain sound technique, but so do the other associated 'S' factors. Repeating a movement over and over will in itself specifically strengthen muscles for that action; develop the particular suppleness to perform it well; improve speed as the efficiency of movement increases; allow it to be used frequently in a game situation without deterioration in quality and thereby produce a technically sound and effective technique. When asked what is the best training for javelin throwing my coach used to say 'throwing the javelin'. All other types of training support this skill-developing process; it should not be seen as the main focus of training.

A major problem arises with the poorly motivated player. For example, some individuals may be so quick at picking up skills that they seem to miss out stages 1 and 2; there is a rapid increase in skill at first which gradually plateaus out – this would equate to Stage 3. At this stage athletes say things like 'Done that, coach, what's next?' or 'I can do this, it's boring.' If they do not persevere and continue the practice they will not ingrain the technique or achieve the associated physical development. Their technique will be erratic and inconsistent because it has not developed the stability associated with stages 4 and 5. Training practices have to be innovative to maintain the interest of the participants to ensure that the benefits of the learning process are maximised. How the coach apportions time to skill development and the strategies available to teach skills will be discussed at length in chapter 12.

(p)Sychology

What makes a champion athlete? The physical qualities needed are self-evident. But what separates the best from the rest? Sports psychology has attempted to identify some of the qualities necessary:

- aggression
- motivation
- determination
- arousal
- self-confidence
- leadership
- mental toughness
- willingness to learn
- desire to win.

No doubt coaches can add to the list.

There is a series of strategies that have been evolved to alleviate stress; improve concentration; adopt an appropriate state of mind; visualise the game; and set goals, among many others. The difficulty arises because in the development of athletes in the main coaches deal with the pre-, peri- and post-pubertal years. The change from childhood to maturity is a hormonally controlled period that greatly affects physique, personality and behaviour. There is evidence to support the theory that more disturbed behaviour is found among teenagers than in any other group. I think that all parents, teachers, coaches and anyone else who lives with or works with this age group have already discovered this!

Csikszentmihalyi has identified that in every culture, adolescence and its associated hormonal influences on brain development and function is an 'explosive package'. He goes on to suggest that this time of life is characterised by anxiety and failure to achieve potential due to factors apparently outside the individual's control. Possibly as a result of the anxiety, anger is a common emotion. Conflict situations occur between adolescents and authority figures, such as parents and teachers – and coaches! The commonly held idea that sport can modify some of the more unpleasant aspects of teenage behaviour has limited merit. Since the cause is maturational, in general, the situation has to run its course. But that does not mean that we should not try!

If the majority of the qualities and strategies presented in sports psychology relate to intellectually mature individuals, how applicable are they to the embryonic player? If, as we have seen, that part of the brain that deals with anxiety, arousal, aggression, prioritising, organising strategies for action and identifying the consequences of planning and preparation does not mature until 25, how appropriate is goal-setting, realistically, with an 11-year-old? Because of the maturational dimension of these and other factors, such themes will be developed in a more practical and realistic way in the following chapters.

CHAPTER 6 PERIODISATION OF TRAINING: BASIC CONCEPTS

THE EFFECT OF PHYSICAL ACTIVITY ON PERFORMANCE

The human body is very adaptable to environmental and lifestyle conditions. It is able to meet the demands of physical activity such as sitting, walking, lifting, carrying or running for the bus as part of our normal behaviour. If we seek occasionally to participate in strenuous physical activity it can draw upon physiological reserves to match the effort required. However if we wish to be involved in intensive exercise on a regular basis we have to prepare ourselves better to ensure that the various anatomical and physiological systems can cope with providing the energy and withstanding the increased physical forces. The way in which an athlete responds to these extreme workloads will depend on the state of her or his body systems and ability to work in a co-ordinated manner. A systematic and progressive programme of training carried out conscientiously over a period of weeks, months and years will bring about changes to the body's function. Improvements in sporting performance will be as a result of this long-term preparation. By creating a sport-specific programme that makes progressive demands on anatomical and physiological systems we cause them to become more efficient in responding to increasing workloads.

Not only must coaches be aware of the fundamentals of designing training and competition programmes, they also have to be vigilant as to the actual effectiveness of the work. Constant monitoring will ensure that progress is being made and, where there are problems, allows for a review of the plan and any modifications. There is a great commitment of time and effort made by all, and it is essential performance development strategy is effective and brings about improvements by design, not chance! The coach should have at least a basic understanding of how the major body systems work and adapt to the sporting environment. Appreciating this process will enable the coach to create the specific improvements the individual requires to achieve improvement and reach their potential.

PHYSICAL ACTIVITY AND ADAPTATION

Any desired physiological changes brought about by training are a result of specifically targeting particular parts of the body. Increasing workloads to bring about the desired effect is known as 'stressing'. If a system is exposed to specific stresses over a period of time 'adaptation' will take place, and it will become more effective and efficient.

Adaptation is Stress Specific

Strength training will make a player stronger! It will not develop suppleness or sport-specific skill. Any physical adaptation is highly specific to the way stress is applied. Speed training will make a player move faster! Simplistically muscles, bones, joints, nerves, heart, lungs and energy systems and their integration are modified in the exact manner in which they are used. Any associated improvements will be linked to the stresses applied. As Pindar said, over 2000 years ago: 'Without toil there have triumphed few.' Which might be brought up to date with, 'You don't get anything for nothing.' The harder you work the more you adapt to what you do.

There is a concept of 'cross training' where participation in a specific sport or activity has a positive effect on another. Careful evaluation of the actuality is that if the stress is aimed at a specific component, say general endurance, there may be some carry-over. But sport-specific adaptation will take place only with specific workloads.

Adaptation Takes Place in the Recovery Phase

I never did fully grasp the implication of the notion, 'No pain no gain.' If the suggestion is that improvement occurs during the activity, then it is incorrect. And, that the more intense the demands of participation the greater the adaptation is also incorrect. The simple fact of the matter is that the body's adaptation to intensive physical work occurs in the recovery period that follows. If any body system is stressed above normal levels it becomes more efficient or stronger to enable it to cope better with these increased workloads when next exposed to them. However, any such changes are subtle and it takes many hours of training to see significant changes. Improvements are directly linked to the quality and quantity of work over many weeks or longer.

There is a process of events that produces the adaptation:

- Work
- Fatigue
- Recovery
- Adaptation

This sequence of phases is referred to as 'The Theory of Overcompensation' (figure 6.1), which was introduced in chapter 4.

It is self-evident that sustained periods of intensive physical activity are going to make the player tired. It is all the elements that bring about this feeling of exhaustion known as 'fatigue' that trigger any changes.

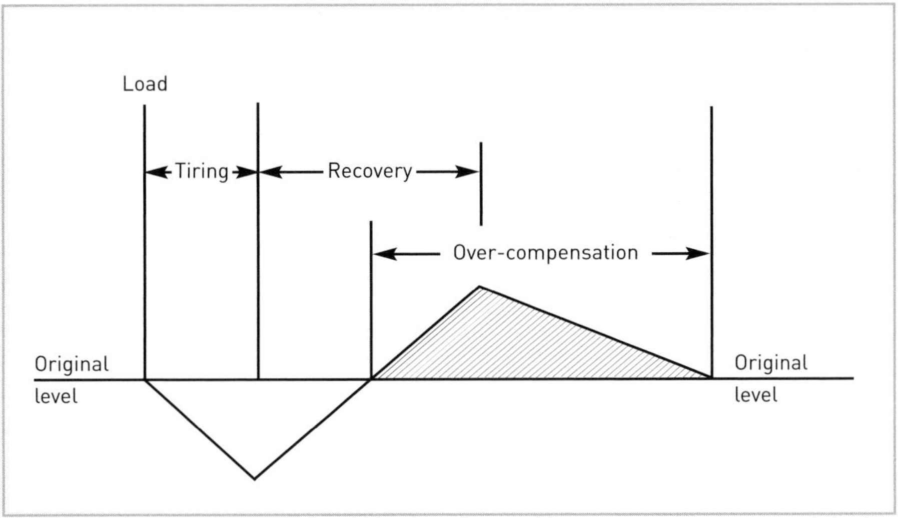

FIG. 6.1 During periods of strenuous physical activity, exercise uses up available and stored reserves of energy and stresses the targeted body systems and tissues. This energy drain and build-up of waste products creates fatigue. In the post-training period, as the athlete recovers energy reserves will be replenished and slightly increased, body tissues will be strengthened and related physiological processes made more efficient.

THE THEORY OF OVERCOMPENSATION

Depletion of Energy Stores

Within the body there are very limited supplies of energy for intense work. These stores, in the form of glycogen, are found primarily in muscle tissue and, to a lesser extent, the liver. There are larger stores of lipids, in the form of body fat, that are used during low-intensity activity, distributed widely throughout each individual. Long-duration low-intensity work sustained for periods of over 30 minutes, such as distance running and cycling, will tend to utilise lipids, and there is an abundance of reserves for this purpose! Most sports and training however are made up of short bursts of intense activity interspaced with less stressful phases or rests. With this type of quality effort the glycogen stores rapidly become depleted, which gives rise to a feeling of tiredness – having little energy!

Accumulation of Waste Products

The various physiological systems within the body are best suited to functioning in an environment with a plentiful supply of oxygen. In a sporting context this is usually referred to as 'aerobic' work. When oxygen is readily available the waste products of physical activity are generally carbon dioxide and water. Circulating blood is an excellent waste removal system and quickly transports these materials away from the areas of production. However, if there is an insufficient supply of oxygen, as in the case of short bursts of very intense activity, this is known as 'anaerobic' work. The main waste product of anaerobic work is lactic acid, which is a viscous product that tends to build up in active areas. The problem arises out of the tendency of the material to clog up active tissue because of its glutinous nature and the fact that the waste transport system is not very efficient at removing it.

If intense activity is sustained for more than a few seconds the lactic acid will quickly build up to a point where it stifles the energy-producing process. Consequently work rate will fall dramatically and performance will deteriorate.

Tissue Breakdown

During physical activity, particularly if it is strenuous, there will be damage to a greater or lesser degree to all the anatomical and physiological systems. DON'T PANIC! This occurs at a cellular, microscopically small, level. Current terminology identifies it as 'micro-trauma'. Basically, in the activity of producing sporting performance, some of the cells of the contributing body organs and systems will become damaged. The number and extent of cells damaged will be related to the intensity of the work, and as training or competition continues there will be a build-up of these microscopic tissue fragments. There may well be an accumulation of this material in active areas and related tissue degradation to a point where performance begins to decline. In extreme cases the localised tissue breakdown may result in an injury, in which case pain and actual damage will prevent further participation and qualified medical advice may be required. The time that tissue needs to repair is related to the amount of cellular degradation.

The Theory of Overcompensation is based on the period following activity. All adaptation takes place in the rest or recovery phase. Following any period of strenuous activity the body has to respond to the after-effects. All the associated waste products that are present in tissues have to be removed. This will include fatigue products such as water, carbon dioxide, lactic acid and the detritus of cellular damage. As this material is removed so the rate of blood-flow into the former sites of activity will increase, which in itself will speed up the process. The inflow of oxygen and nutrients will then enable the recovery phase to develop:

- energy stores will be replenished
- cellular damage will be repaired
- the gas, fuel and waste transport systems recover.

The body's response to this situation is to take a very pragmatic approach – it adapts! Since it was not able to meet the demands made on various systems it attempts to make sure that the same thing does not happen again. It:

- overfills the energy reserves
- repairs cellular damage and strengthens the associated tissue
- makes the transport system more efficient.

It takes time for all these processes to be completed, hours or even days depending upon the amount of repair, refilling and modifications. Obviously changes are infinitesimally small following each session but over a period of time improvements will become manifest and with a progressive training programme will continue. It is this simple cycle of events that happens at a microscopic level that is the basis for creating champions.

The Cycle of Overcompensation is the 'engine' that creates the progressive improvement in overall performance. The coach has to be aware of the subtleties of the elements that make up that process:

Specificity

The training for any sport must reflect the specific technical and tactical demands of that sport. It is self-evident that the development of skills in rugby will require a considerable amount of time being allocated to sport-specific activities such as handling, passing, running, tackling, kicking and catching. The coach may also wish to develop individual positional requirements in both attack and defence. Periods during practices set aside for five-a-side football will not contribute to improvements in skill levels.

Planning training over a period of time can be a daunting task and sometimes in the haste to include every possible element an imbalance can occur. For example, strength training is an important aspect of preparation for most sports, but it must be directed and appropriate. A general programme will have limited effect on performance. What kind of strength does the sport need? Explosive and maximal against an external object such as in the case of a forward in a scrum, or sustained and low level such as dribbling with the ball in soccer. Developing one kind of strength will not improve the other. There is the case of David Beckham who claimed that a loss of form was due to an overemphasis on gym work that caused him to gain weight. This increase in bodyweight reduced his mobility and general coordination, and the result was impaired performance. Yes, he had been training hard, putting in the hours of intense work, but the result was the exact opposite of his intention. Hours of effort do not equate with improvement! Adaptation is specific to the stress applied.

Overload

Once the coach has decided which element of strength, speed, suppleness, stamina, strength or skill needs developing, the specific parts of the body that are used need to be identified and stressed in similar manner. If this work can be undertaken relatively easily with little effort it is unlikely that adaptation will occur. If a high jumper can easily raise their lead knee to waist height and does so in any number of practices it will not give the required range of movement necessary to reach chest height: a refinement of skill is required for excellence. Specific isolation exercises that target the limbs and joints are needed. During such activity the range of movement over a period of time will be taken to the end point of the normal range and gently beyond. This will give rise to the improvements necessary, for instance, in knee lift.

If any system is used within the normal range or demands of training or competition no improvement will take place. The coach has to be conscious to increase loads gradually, because adaptive processes take place slowly. Too great an increase in loads will not bring about a commensurate improvement. It is more likely to cause injury or an overlong period of recovery, both of which have the same deleterious effect upon performance.

Intensity

The Theory of Overcompensation requires body systems to be loaded above that which they are exposed to in normal life or in the rigours of training or competition, for the adaptive processes to take place. The difficulty for the coach is to assess the correct loadings. Any training programme must be tailored to meet the exact requirements of each athlete. With individual activities such as swimming this is relatively straightforward but with team sports such as hockey, not only the individual must be considered but specific positional needs as well. Team practices where everyone does the same training are not an effective way of ensuring individual development.

Team training indicates the difficulties in judging the workloads. The session has to be pitched at the average level of ability. For the 'average' player the intensity of work will be appropriate to produce positive changes. But, those with a higher fitness level should have more demanding work to improve. And, for the unfit the training will be too much, to the extent that injury may be a possibility and the recovery process from almost 'shock loadings' will take many days and preclude any further physical activity. Generalised group training will not produce the optimum conditions for the adaptive processes and few if any will maximise their improvement.

Progression

The overcompensation from a single training session is infinitesimally small. Progression is achieved over a sustained period of time and only by training on a regular basis, often daily and perhaps more than one session a day. Any increase in workload should only occur when tissues have adapted to the existing levels. Coaches must realise that there is no wonder programme that can produce meteoric improvements in a short time-frame. Any attempt to increase loadings before the previous ones have been fully accommodated, or too great a progression, can create the potential for injuries or worse. The adaptive process is slow. For significant physical changes to be measured it is suggested that six weeks is the *minimum* time-frame. Increases in workloads must be gradual, any enthusiasm to gain or regain sporting proficiency must be tempered with caution, common sense and an understanding of the processes involved.

Frequency

There are times, such as with an important match, when extra practice sessions are organised to prepare the squad better. But, as with many things in life, more is not always better! Overload, intensity, progression, and frequency should be appropriate to the aptitude of the player. Fitter players will generally recover faster from training while the less well conditioned will take longer. If both are subjected to the same time-frame, and, perhaps, workload the ones with lower fitness levels will not recover at the same rate and will probably be in a poor state for the game!

One of the benefits of the Theory of Overcompensation is that not only do related tissues adapt progressively but the very processes involved become more efficient and operate in a faster time-scale. The fitter you are the faster you recover. The faster you recover the sooner you are ready to train again! Most elite athletes over a long period of time will build up from two or three days of activity a week, to four, five, six or seven. At elite levels their rapid recovery rates enable them to train once, twice or more often a day.

When devising a training schedule the fitness level of the athlete is a very important consideration. It will dictate the workload and the time it takes to recover such that the next session occurs at the optimum time (figure 6.2). If the time between sessions is insufficient for full recovery or too long, the rate of improvement will be compromised at best. Many athletes fail to reach their potential because they do not fully appreciate the need to train on a regular basis over a considerable period of time. The commitment of the athlete must match the planning and input of the coach.

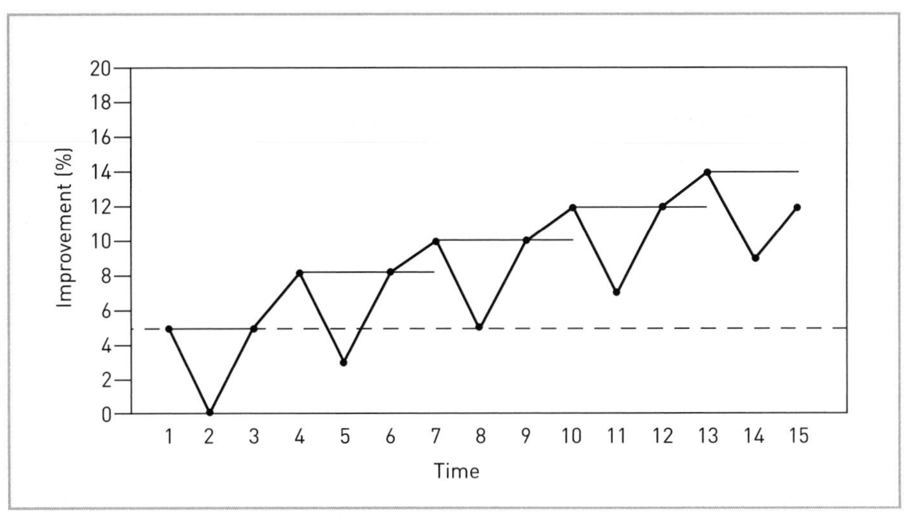

FIG. 6.2 The systematic planning of training is essential to ensure the benefits of over-compensation are maximised. If succssive physical activity coincides with these peaks on a regular basis, the elements of fitness targeted and the athlete's performance will improve in a progressive manner.

CHAPTER 7 PLANNING THE PROGRAMME: APPLYING THE THEORY

The universe in which we exist, the galaxies, stars, planets and the vast range of celestial bodies that contribute to the whole seem to have a natural rhythm. The ancients gave it a name: 'the dance of the celestial spheres'. Our own solar system has its own rhythm which manifests on earth as the yearly cycle, made up of sub-units comprising the four seasons; summer, autumn, winter and spring. Within the yearly cycle also exists the monthly lunar phasing. Within each month there are four seven-day weeks. Each 24 hours has its own cycle of night and day. Adaptation of human beings to these natural cycles has resulted in their being better suited to activity in daylight and being more active in summer than winter. Not only do these rhythms markedly affect our lifestyle, they influence sporting performance.

CONSTRUCTING A TRAINING PROGRAMME

When beginning to construct a training programme the coach has to consider a range of variables.

Time of Day

Lifestyles tend to prescribe the amount of time that can be given over to sport and training. The time of day training or competition takes place can affect the adaptive process. Most sports matches take place on weekend afternoons. History has given rise to the fact that mid-afternoon is the best time. Recent research supports the idea that the body is best suited for strenuous physical activity between 1.00 and 4.00 pm. It follows that this is the best time for training. Competitions and training, however, do have to take place at other times. The implication is that the body is not at its best! Most training takes place after school, work and daily commitments. Loadings need to consider this notion and be monitored carefully. The rate of progress is affected by the timing of sessions. The optimum times of day for physical sysems are:

Brain function	1.00 pm
Body temperature	3.00 pm
Heart rate	4.00 pm
Respiration	2.30 pm
Total body efficiency	3.30 pm

Frequency of Sessions

How does the coach identify the period between training sessions to optimise progression? In the 1950s the German scientist Hans Selye produced his 'General Adaptation to Stress Theory' (GAS). Selye discovered that people involved in strenuous physical activity for a prolonged period of time achieved their best possible rate of improvement if they were stressed at approximately 80 per cent of their maximum (figure 7.1). This figure can vary on a week-to-week or month-to-month basis but over the whole time-scale, say a training year, it would average at 80 per cent (figure 7.2). It is suggested that loadings for younger athletes might be lower than 80 per cent increasing as maturity and conditioning develop.

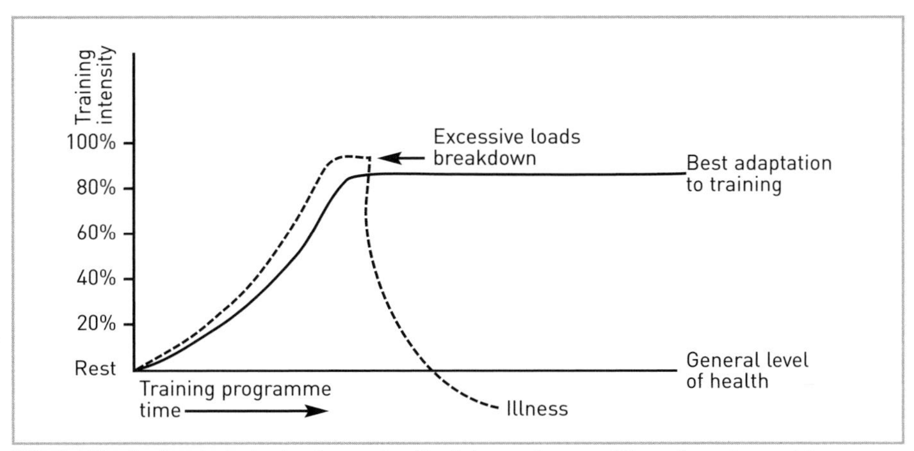

FIG. 7.1 The body adapts to the demands of training and competition when stressed to approximately 80 per cent of maximum. If loadings are sustained beyond this level, breakdown and illness will occur.

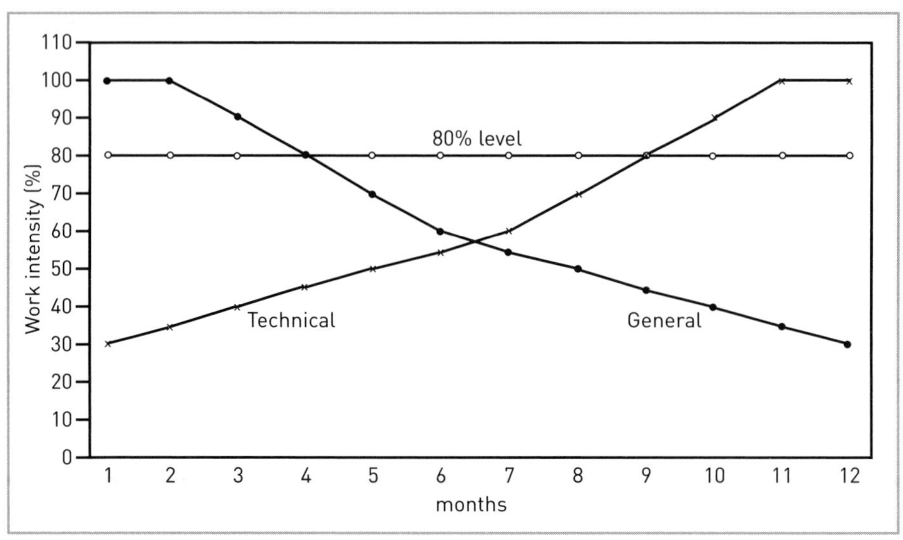

FIG. 7.2 Carefully planned training will enable an athlete to maintain an overall standard of performance of 80 per cent throughout the year. Levels of 100 per cent, or more, can only be sustained for a short period, approximately six weeks in 12 months. It is essential that the balance of technical and general training is planned to coincide with specific events.

The GAS theory might seem to contradict the Theory of Overcompensation, but in fact it maximises its function in the simple fact that all training sessions are not identical. Athletics training, for example, tends to be more intense in the winter, the preparation phase, than in the summer, the competition phase (figure 7.3). A weekly schematic for a young shot putter in summer might be as follows:

Saturday	Competition (100 per cent)
Sunday	Technical session working on specific aspects of technique and/or particular aspects noted in Saturday's competition (50 per cent)
Monday	Strength training – general (100 per cent)
Tuesday	Technical session (80 per cent)
Wednesday	Strength training – shot-specific (100 per cent)
Thursday	Technical session – competition-specific (80 per cent)
Friday	Light jogging/mobility (50 per cent)

It can be seen that each day has a different form of training and intensity of working. Not all sessions are maximal, there are hard days interspersed with easier

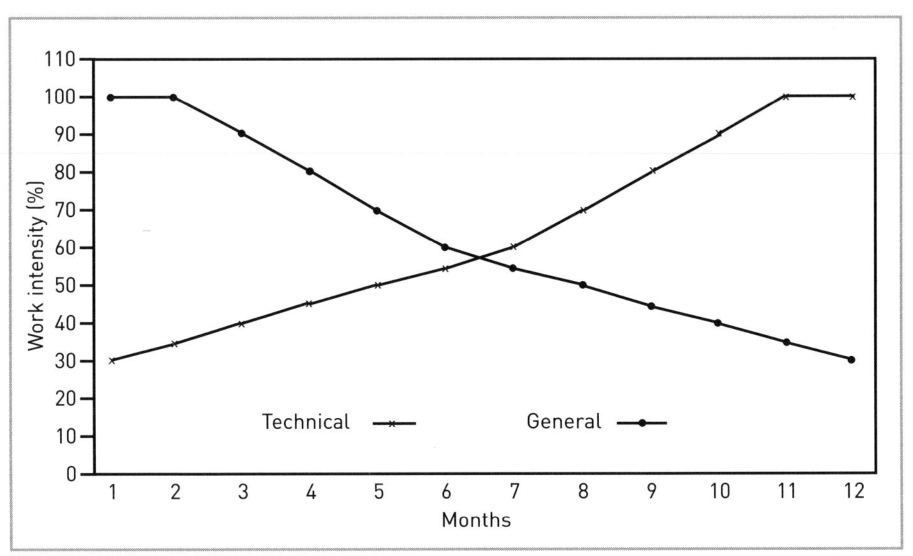

FIG. 7.3 The nature of training for a shot putter shifts from conditioning to technical and competition-specific work in the spring and summer.

days. I have attempted to indicate the intensity of each session in percentages of maximum effort needed to carry out each day's activities. The total is 560 per cent over seven days, which is an average of 80 per cent per day, as Selye suggested, the loadings being appropriate to the time of year and the physical development of the athlete. Each day's work emphasises a different type of training, which utilises the integration of body systems in highly distinctive ways. This ensures that systems are not worked at maximal levels on successive days allowing for the overcompensation cycle to operate efficiently and effectively. Figure 7.4 shows how the related theory fits into a periodised year, and identifies the need to sequence training sessions to maximise the training effect.

Planning the Training Year

As an athletics coach I have been asked on countless occasions by schools, parents and coaches if I could 'work with' their talented youngsters. This usually happens two weeks before a major schools competition! Though I am generally happy to make general observations it would be disastrous to make changes in such a short time-frame. The reality is these embryonic stars have followed no systematic preparation and it is actually believed that one or two sessions will elevate them from an adequate performance to national champions. Oh that it was so easy!

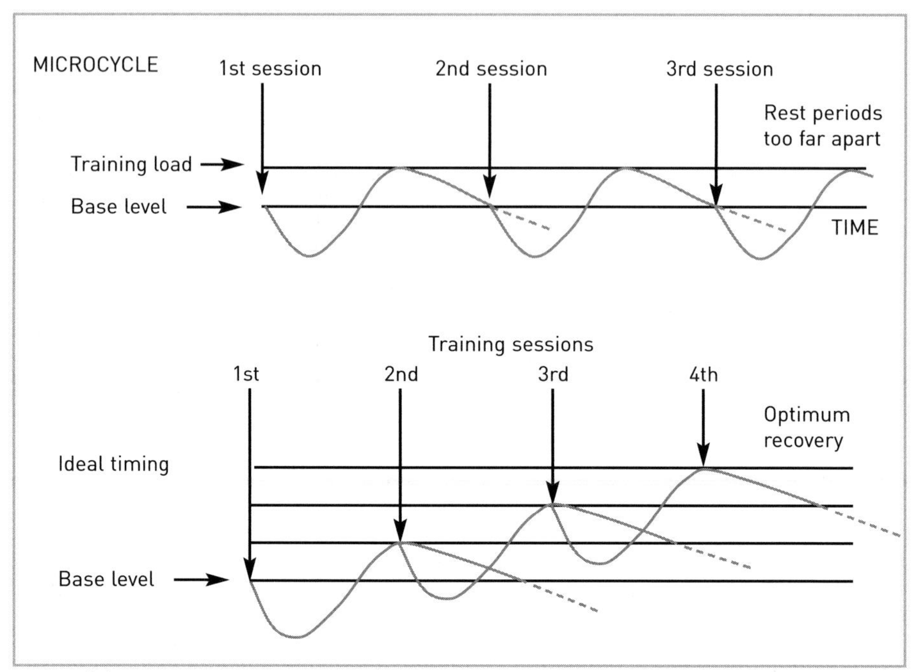

FIG. 7.4(a) The importance of timing successive training sessions to optimise the adaptive process

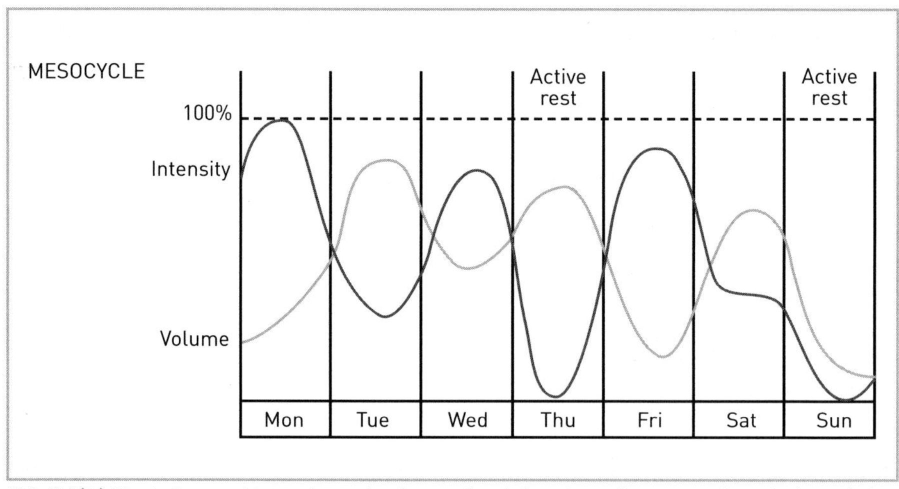

FIG. 7.4(b) The balance of intensity and volume of training throughout a week period needed to meet Selye's recommendations

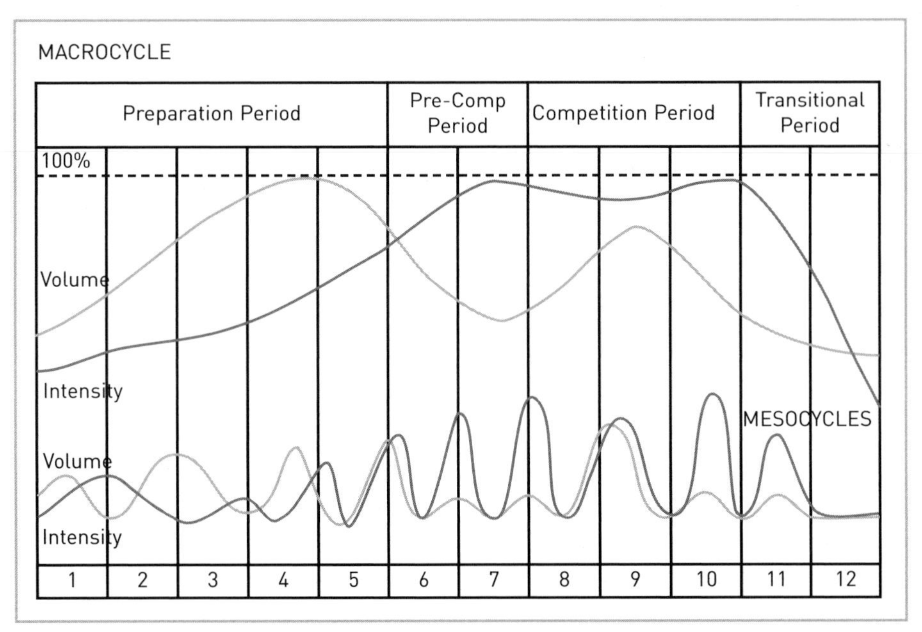

FIG. 7.4(c) The periodised year, with monthly training loads suggested that contribute to the annual programme. Maximal performance in any year can only be sustained for a limited period of about six weeks. In this example, a double peak, each of three weeks is presented.

'Great Oaks from little acorns grow.' Elite performance at any level occurs through careful planning and the hard work of the athlete and all concerned, not by chance. The coach has to design a programme of training that considers, among other components:

- the competition period – summer, winter or all year round
- league fixtures or competitions
- priorities of specific events
- holidays
- facilities available
- time of training.

This information will enable the coach to plan out a detailed and comprehensive schedule of fixtures and the necessary preparation required to achieve success (figure 7.5).

Month – Week commencing																																																				
Week training year	1	2	3	4	5	6	7	8	9	10	11	12	13	14	15	16	17	18	19	20	21	22	23	24	25	26	27	28	29	30	31	32	33	34	35	36	37	38	39	40	41	42	43	44	45	46	47	48	49	50	51	52

Planned competition/Grading programme		
Date	Venue	Competition/Grading

Notes

FIG. 7.5 A year planner is useful when identifying fixtures, major dates and loadings.

The year can be simplistically divided into five parts:

1 **The preparation phase**. This the non-competitive period of the year. For a novice it is the start of the preparation for the competition and games that lie a long way ahead. It is the foundation for all the subsequent work. It is characterised by general conditioning and the reinforcement of general skills. For the experienced player it is a time to work on aspects of technique and general areas of performance that may need particular attention before the next phase. The emphasis of training is on fitness not technical excellence.

2 **The transition or pre-season phase**. With most sports this period begins approximately eight weeks before the main competition period. The emphasis in training changes from the general to the specific. Because of the thorough preparation of all of the contributory body systems they can now be loaded towards the very specific demands of the sport and any positional requirements. The previous focus on general fitness levels allows for more emphasis on technical and tactical preparation.

3 **The early competitive season**. From the start of the season training is geared towards the requirement of the sport. General fitness work is directed towards maintaining levels of conditioning. Training emphasises the physical, technical and tactical demands. During practices individuals are subjected to the demands of competiton to prepare them for the physical and mental rigours of the real thing. The coach might consider reducing the number of training sessions in this period to allow for effective recovery.

4 **The competitive phase**. This period can be organised to last for a sustained period or two shorter ones; the coach has to identify the athlete's and her or his own priorities. Training is modified to enable specific aspects of performance to be evaluated and worked on. Herb Elliott, the great world-class distance runner, said that competition was the best form of training; during this period preparation supports performance. The balance of training and competition has to be balanced to maintain Selye's optimum stress levels.

5 **The recovery phase**. Just as important as all the other phases is the period between the end of the competition period and the start of preparations for the next. The body and the mind have been subjected to intensive work for a considerable period of time. Every body system needs to recuperate. This time in the sporting year is often referred to as 'active rest'. It should not be a period of total inactivity. Athletes should be encouraged to participate in other sports and

recreational activities not just for pleasure but to maintain a basic level of fitness which will be the base-line for the next season's training. Many sports set out basic fitness levels such as the number of press-ups and sit-ups in a minute or a minimum time for a run of 3000 metres. This ensures that fitness levels do not fall too low and require remedial measures at the start of the training period.

Undertraining

Selye's research identified the fact that if the workload was insufficient or that there was too much recovery or rest between sessions there would not be an improvement in performance (figure 7.4(a)). That in itself can be problematical for the coach in balancing the variables, but by constantly monitoring the programme and reviewing progress regularly modifications can be made to rectify the situation. How each individual responds to a schedule is unique. Two equally talented youngsters in every respect can both follow the same programme to the letter and improve at different rates. Though the effects are by and large predictable, planning training is not an exact science, which is a fact that parents, coaches and others involved forget at times.

Overtraining

Sport and training account for only a part of the lifestyle of a young player. Other elements include family and social life and work or school. Selye identified that all can be stressful in their own way. He went on to describe how all these factors affect the individual. One of the key aspects of his theory was that he did not differentiate between physical and mental stress, they were inextricably linked. He said that all activity requires fuel which we obviously obtain from the food we eat. He identified four areas that draw on this energy source.

1. General body maintenance, growth, resistance to infection and repair of tissue damage – especially of that due to sport
2. Family and social life
3. Work or school
4. Sports training

Simplistically, in a well-balanced lifestyle, each element should have an equal share of the energy pie, 25 per cent each (figure 7.6(a)). An imbalance in any one will have a detrimental effect on one or more of the others.

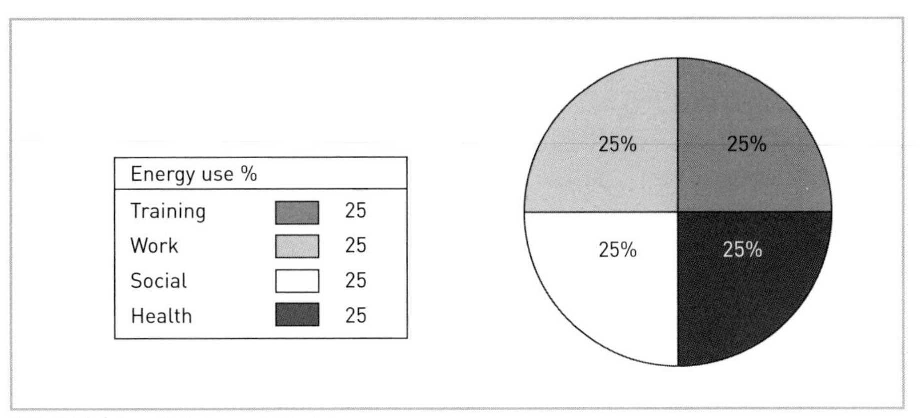

FIG. 7.6(a) A well-balanced lifestyle

If the training load is too intense or the involvement in sport becomes excessive it is going to need additional energy to fuel the associated activity. The other elements have to operate on reduced rations. Increasing fuel intake will not resolve this apportioning of reserves. More time in sport means less time and success in family, social, work and school involvement. More importantly, as fuel is drawn away from the body's maintenance system, recovery from training will take longer (figure 7.6(b)). Less energy will give a feeling of being constantly tired. The immune system is compromised and colds and minor infections are easily picked up. *The coach and/or parents need to quickly revise the overall programme at the onset of such a situation.*

The lack in sports performance might be met with even more time being given to sport at the expense of the rest. Overall lifestyle starts to fall apart, there is a

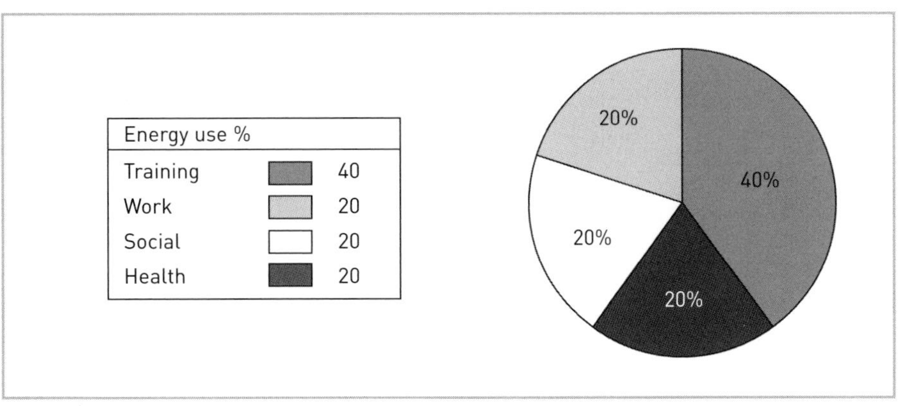

FIG. 7.6(b) The onset of overtraining

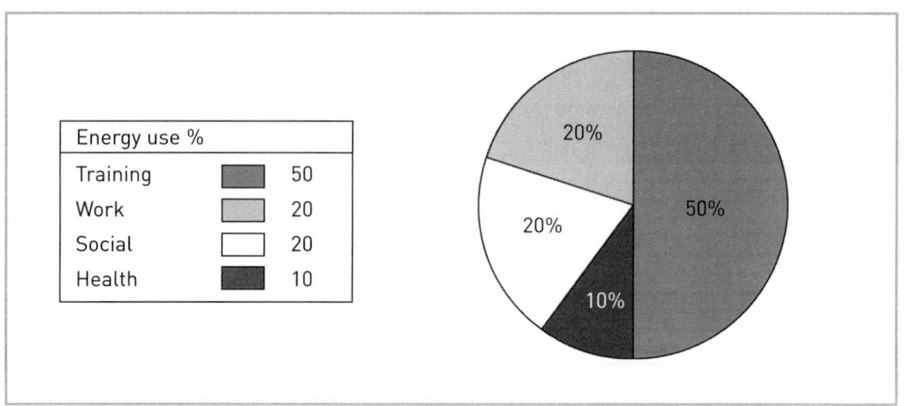

FIG. 7.6(c) By this stage, chronic overtraining is giving rise to injury and ill health.

constant feeling of intense fatigue, illnesses become more serious and, of course, all sporting activities begin to self-destruct and injuries become common (figure 7.6(c)). *Radical measures must to be actioned .*

Without interventions the process spirals down with greater destructive effect. At this stage the effects of overtraining are self-evident. Relationships suffer or break down, school or work deteriorates, disastrous sporting performances are the norm. Mental dysfunction often occurs to compound the declining physical and sporting situation. *At this stage any recovery strategy may be beyond the ability of the coach or parent and medical advice might be sought.*

The responsibility of parents and coaches is to ensure that any involvement in sport is enjoyable and enables each participant to achieve his or her potential. It is also to protect them from harm. The monitoring of a training programme is not just to check on its effectiveness, but also to allow for those involved to obtain an overview of the individual's response to it. Any indications of deteriorating performance must be reviewed and causes identified and acted on. Any signs of obsessive attitudes towards sport by the youngster or those who have influence over her or him must be addressed at the outset.

Determining the Training Load

For a coach the evaluation of training loads is one of the most difficult tasks. It is the assessment of the technical, tactical and physical workloads which is at the heart of performance development and coaching champions. The most difficult aspect is the initial identification of loadings for a novice just beginning the long haul to success, quite simply because there is nothing on which to base a judgement. Once the process is established the coach has a record of previous programmes, workloads and tests to assess 'S' factor components and, importantly, competition performances for reference.

Initially there is a multitude of variables that need to be considered, which must start with basic details:

- chronological age
- sex
- talent
- aspirations
- coachability
- determination
- positive home environment
- time available for training.

How then should the coach begin the process?

1 Temper enthusiasm with caution! It is wiser to set lower training intensities rather than excessive ones. The player will be able to meet the demands of training and playing comfortably and will rapidly recover for the next period of activity. Signs of an insufficient workload include:

- finishing drills and activities faster than expected
- standing about
- interfering with others still training
- wandering off
- loss of concentration
- becoming bored
- frustration with lack of challenging work
- losing interest in the proceedings.

By constantly monitoring the situation, loadings can be tweaked and gently increased to optimum levels for the benefit of all concerned.

2 With some sports such as track, field and swimming it is relatively straightforward to obtain competition performances and devise initial programmes. With other sports such as football and basketball, performance tends to be more subjective. Most governing bodies provide technique evaluation details for coaches, which can readily provide a technical evaluation. There are range skill drill tests, which can be used to assess and monitor performance. Experienced coaches tend to personalise tests to meet the athlete's and their own specific requirements.

There is a wide range of general and sport-specific exercises that the coach can use to develop 'S' factors in an appropriate manner for the individual and the sport or positional demands. It is essential that a detailed record of test and training marks and workloads should be kept and used as part of the monitoring and review process.

3 There are other visual indicators that can give the coach an indication of the player's response to a session (table 7.1):

VISUAL INDICATORS OF A PLAYER'S RESPONSE TO A TRAINING SESSION **TABLE 7.1**

	UNDERTRAINING	IDEAL TRAINING	OVERTRAINING
Skin	Normal	A healthy pink	Deep red
Sweating	None	Profuse in upper body	Profuse throughout the body
Skill	No deterioration	Deteriorates as session progresses	Breaks down, lacks coordination
Mental focus	Lack of attention	Concentration deteriorates as session progresses	Brief periods of concentration
Health	No change	Fatigue develops as session progresses	Pains in muscles, joints and other areas
Commitment to training	Bored and frustrated	Enthusiastic	Needs more time to recover, anxiety felt towards training and performance

CHAPTER 8
ASSESSING PERFORMANCE

When devising a sport-specific training programme for an athlete the coach needs to identify a base level of ability. From this assessment a schedule of work can be created that is appropriate to the individual. This initial evaluation can also be used to monitor the effectiveness of the training as the plan unfolds. There is a need for constant evaluation of the programme to ensure that any training resources are optimised. There is a cycle of operations that should be completed at regular intervals:

- Assess – the individual's ability.
- Plan – a training programme.
- Prepare – ensure that equipment, facilities and other resources are available.
- Deliver – run the session.
- Record – how did it go? Did it work? Good/bad points?
- Monitor – are there improvements? Yes/no? Where?
- Assess – the individual's ability.
- Modify – does the programme need changing – if so how?
- Implement – the changes.

The assessment of an individual's ability can be broken down into two broad areas:

1 technical and tactical sport-specific skills and their application
2 fitness which is sport- and position-specific.

Most governing bodies of sport produce assessment tests for their own sports, often linked to an award scheme. Schools link into these schemes to encourage youngsters to develop skills to 'win' a badge or certificate. How these pupils go on to utilise these abilities within sport is then, unfortunately, less clear. Many sports claim tens of thousands of award winners which in itself is meritorious but bears no resemblance whatsoever to the number of those involved in competitive sport outside of the school lesson. I would encourage coaches to look at the assessment activities which their governing body suggests. However, it may well be that the coaches wish to be selective as to the ones that are appropriate for their situation. Often, experienced coaches devise their own tests to identify particular elements of performance they feel are appropriate or essential, the Jumping and Throwing Decathlons devised by Wilf Paish are typical of such innovative practice.

Tests that sports use are in the main not new. Many have been around for time out of mind and now surface to perform specific tasks. In point of fact many sports use the same tests, as with Wilf's. I have selected examples of tests and measures that I have found of value and those used by other coaches, many of which have been personalised to meet the reality of the training or competition requirements. I have also selected tests that not only produce valuable information to the coach but are also simple to use – not everyone has access to sports science laboratories. It is interesting to note that very often recourse to the sports sciences seeks only to confirm the practical coach's assessment. The normal contents of the coach's sports bag, stopwatch, tape measure, whistle and readily available sport-specific equipment should be sufficient to organise and measure the tests. Recent research from America suggests that laboratory-based tests that require sophisticated equipment, are expensive to run and have limited access may not be as accurate and infallible as previously thought. 'Field tests' organised by the coach can be at least as accurate, are much easier to implement and entail no cost. If possible, tests and retests should be performed in similar conditions to ensure comparability of results.

The tests attempt to evaluate the two elements of performance, skill and fitness.

1 Skill. Any gym-type tests can only reflect elements of the actual competitive situation, they are not the real thing. Dribbling around cones is not the same as trying to weave your way through an opponent's defence. Cones don't tackle! The coach has to use or devise tests that reflect as closely as possible specific parts of the game and do so in such a way that they can be repeated easily and accurately when required. That tests can be repeated in the same way is essential if the results of a drill are to be compared with subsequent ones as part of the review process, or so that the results of one player can be compared on the same basis as those of another player.

2 Fitness. The same is true with tests that evaluate the 'S' factors. They have to be sport-specific. Running a 1500-metre time trial will not give much information to the coach of a weightlifter! Tests must as closely as possible mirror and measure the demands of the sport or position.

SKILL TESTS

Association Football

1 DRIBBLING THE BALL

Mark out with cones a start and finish line, 10 m apart (figure 8.1). The player stands with a ball at his or her feet behind the start line. On the command 'Go!' or whistle blast, the player runs, dribbling the ball, as fast as he or she can, in as near a straight line as possible, towards and across the finish line. The activity is timed.

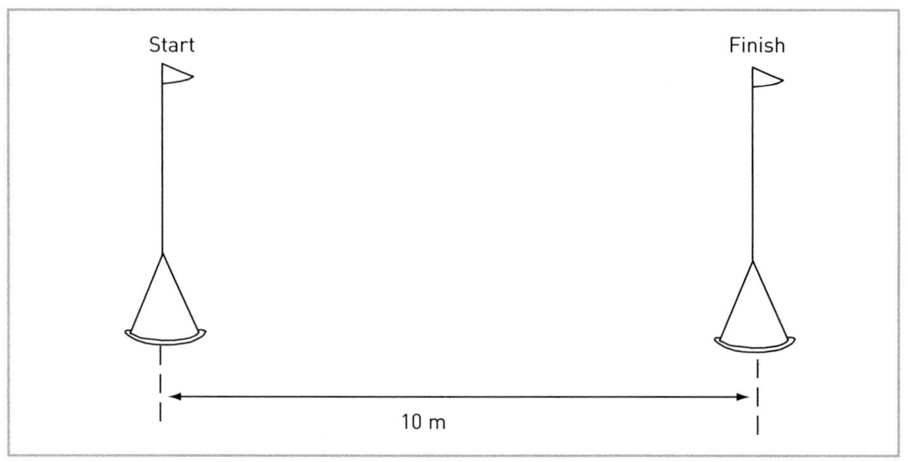

FIG. 8.1 The player dribbles the ball as quickly as possible from the start to finish.

* The activity can be repeated/modified using distances of between 10 and 50 metres. The coach can specify dribbling with right or left foot, which will identify a player's dominant side and therefore the one to be developed, or both feet, which will spotlight control, coordination and balance.

COACHING TIP
You can have the player under test run on a pitch or court marking line. This will enable the coach to assess the degree of control and speed in a straight line.

2 DRIBBLING WITH THE BALL AROUND CONES

Mark out two lines, 15 m apart, with cones set at 3 m intervals, starting with timing as test 1 (figure 8.2). Dribbling the ball and moving as quickly as possible, the player weaves his or her way through the cones.

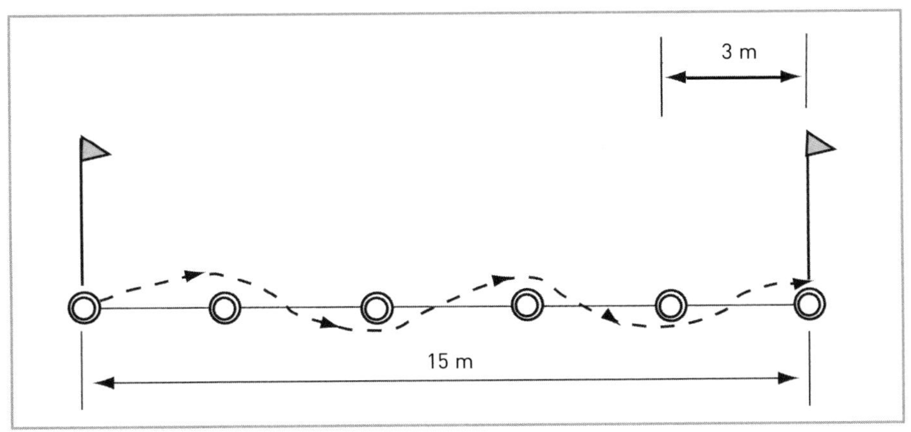

FIG. 8.2 Dribbling around cones

* The activity can be repeated/modified using greater or lesser distances between lines and cones. The closer the cones the greater the ball control. The coach can specify whether to pass the cone on the right or the left, which again will identify the weaker side, or to alternate, which will spotlight control, coordination and balance. An option is to dribble there and back, which will increase the difficulty of the drill.

COACHING TIP
Again the test can be organised with the cones on a line. This will indicate to the coach how close a player is to the cone.

3 TURNING WITH THE BALL

Set out 4 cones in the form of a square with diagonals of 10 m; a further cone is placed at their intersection. Starting and timing is as before. Standing at the centre, cone 5, the player dribbles towards cone 1, turns around it, heads towards cone 3, turns around that one towards the middle. At the centre she or he turns through 90 degrees and runs towards cone 4 goes round it and back towards cone 2, round it and runs to the centre to finish (figure 8.3).

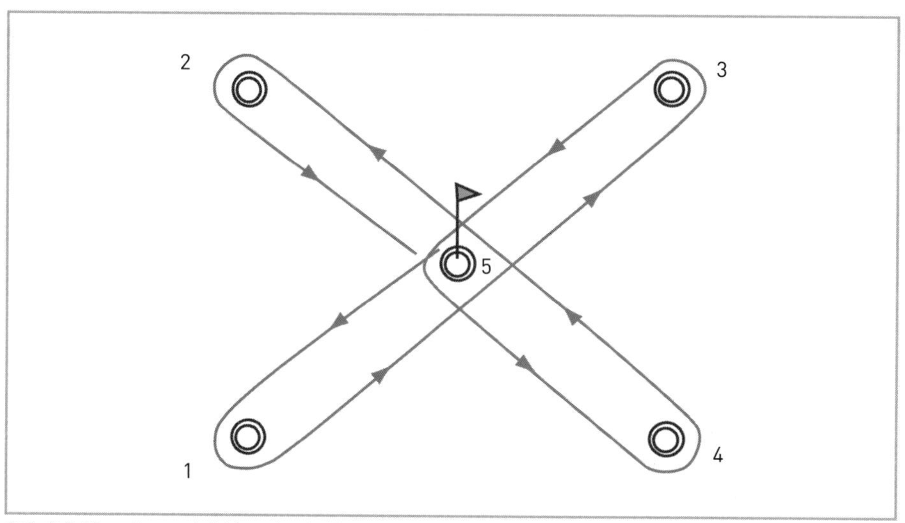

FIG. 8.3 The player dribbles the ball around cones 1, 3, 4 and 2 back to the finish.

* The activity can be repeated/modified with greater or lesser distances between the cones. The coach can specify whether to turn to the left or the right. The times of a circuit of right turns compared to one of left turns will indicate the weaker side. Alternating turns will spotlight control, co-ordination and balance.

COACHING TIP

The coach can specify which turning technique is to be used, for instance the Kruyff Turn. Again this will give an indication of which skills are competently performed and those that need attention.

4 SHOOTING AT GOAL

Position 2 cones 3 m apart as a goal; to indicate start and shooting position, one cone is placed 5 m from goal and a second 10 m behind that (figure 8.4). The player starts at cone 1, dribbles to 2 and shoots at goal. The player has ten attempts.

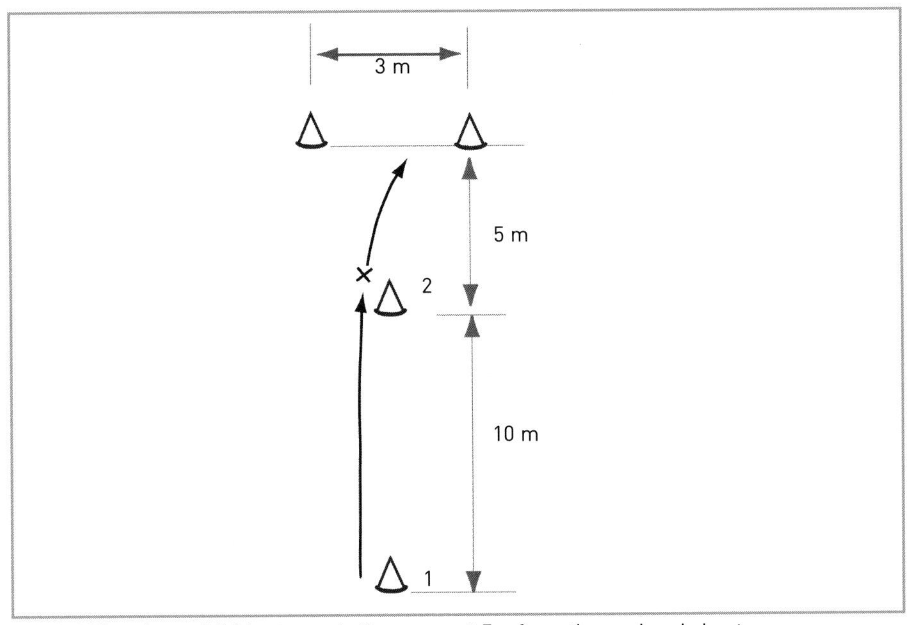

FIG. 8.4 The player dribbles towards the cone set 5m from the goal and shoots.

* The activity can be repeated/modified by moving the shooting mark closer or further away from goal. The cones can be positioned centrally directly in front of goal or to the right or left at specific distances, the coach should keep a record of the exact details. The coach can specify which foot to shoot from, which will indicate the less favoured side.

COACHING TIP
Most players have a dominant shooting foot and favoured side of goal to strike from. By placing the cones at wider intervals from the central line and specifying which foot to shoot with an accurate picture of strengths and weaknesses will be gained.

5A PASSING (1)

Use a wall and a cone. Position the cone 5 m from wall (figure 8.5). Player stands at the side of the cone facing the wall, passes the ball to the wall, traps the rebound and repeats. The coach times ten attempts. Inaccurate passing will take longer!

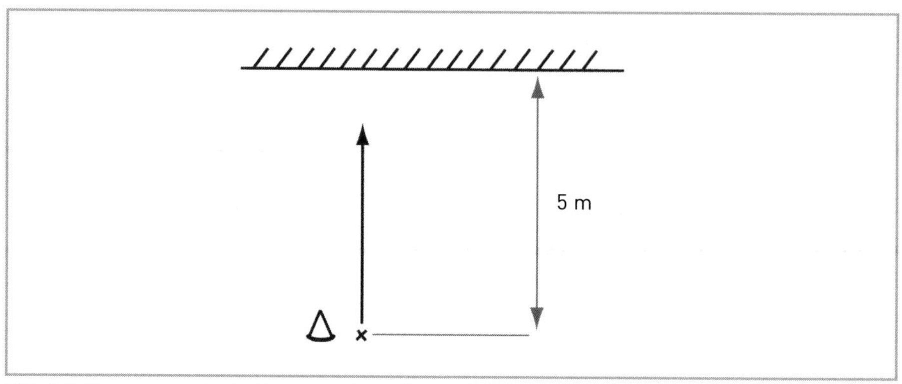

FIG. 8.5 The player stands 5 m away from the wall, passes and recovers the ball and repeats the sequence 10 times as quickly as possible.

* The activity can be repeated/modified by varying the distance between the cone and wall.

5B PASSING (2)

Using the same goal set-up as test 4 a cone is set 20 m away. The player has ten attempts to pass the ball through the cones. The coach records the successful ones.
* The activity can be repeated/modified by varying the distance from the cone to the target. The distance between the goal cones can be altered to vary the difficulty of the test. The coach must keep exact details. The coach can specify which foot is to be used.

COACHING TIP
By assessing the success of right and left foot passing at various distances the coach can evaluate specific strengths and weaknesses.

6 HEADING THE BALL

The player stands 3 m from the coach or assistant, who gently throws the ball so that it falls towards the head of the player. The ball is headed back towards the 'feeder'. The coach times ten attempts. Inaccurate heading will take longer!

* The activity can be repeated/modified varying the distance between the player and feeder. The position of the player can be changed so as to be facing, or with right or left side towards the feeder.

COACHING TIP

Most players have a favoured side when heading the ball. By varying the test the coach can assess specific strengths and weaknesses.

Rugby Football Union and League

7 RUNNING WITH THE BALL

Organised as test 1. The coach can specify if the ball is held in the right or left hand. They can also specify a normal running action or if the free arm is held up to protect the player and/or ball.

COACHING TIP
As for test 1.

8 EVADING TACKLES (1) The Body Swerve

Organised as test 2. Choice of hand in which to hold the ball and the side to pass the cone can be dictated by the coach.

9 EVADING TACKLES (2) The Side-Step

Organised as above.

- The player feints right and goes left, or vice versa.
- Feints left, goes left, or vice versa.
- Feints left, feints right, goes left, or vice versa.
- Any variations on the theme.

COACHING TIP
As for test 2.

10 TURNING WITH THE BALL (1)

Organised as tests 3 and 8.

COACHING TIP
As for tests 3 and 8.

11 TURNING WITH THE BALL (2) Pick Up and Put Down

Organised as above. After turning around the first cone the ball is placed near the central cone, without any change in pace. The player heads for the next cone, turns around that one and runs back to the centre, this time picking the ball up. The drill continues with the player alternately placing and picking up the ball at the centre until the test is completed.

COACHING TIPS
As for tests 3 and 8.

12 PASSING

Organise as test 6. The feeder in this drill passes the ball to the player who in turn passes to another player 3 m distant. The activity can be repeated/modified by varying the distance between the passer and receiver. The position of the player can be changed so that they receive facing, or with right or left side towards the feeder. The player has ten attempts.

COACHING TIP
As for test 5.

13 CATCHING

Organise as test 6. The player has ten attempts. The activity can be repeated/ modified as with tests 6 and 10.

COACHING TIP
The feeder can change the flight of a ball to mimic a kick, a knee-level or normal pass, or any variation on the theme.

14 RECOVERING FOLLOWING A TACKLE

Place two cones 5 m apart. The player runs towards the second cone, lies down full length, rolls sideways through 360 degrees, stands up and runs back to the start. The coach times ten attempts.

COACHING TIP
The coach can designate which way to roll and the distance to run.

With a grasp of the basic principles of organisation most sports can be reduced to a handful of basic tests that can give the coach valuable data. For example:

Basketball

- dribbling the ball (in a straight line) using left, right or alternate hands
- dribbling using cones
- passing using specified techniques
- shooting at goal using specified techniques.

Individual sports can be assessed using the same concepts:

Tennis

- speed of movement around the court (similar to test 3 using court markings)
- serve – to forehand court for accuracy – score out of 10 serves
- serve – to backhand court for accuracy – score out of 10 serves
- backhand return –score out of 10 serves
- forehand return – score out of 10 serves.

Many other sports such as swimming, track and field, cycling, canoeing, skiing and endurance have a specific measurement of time, height or distance in competition or training that give explicit objective information. All sports to a greater or lesser degree have a technical component, the correct way of doing something, which constantly needs to be monitored. Some activities, such as gymnastics and diving, have a major artistic or aesthetic component within the competition structure. The technical and tactical elements of physical activities in both the competition and training environment might additionally be served with the use of video analysis of performance.

FITNESS TESTS

Everyone needs to develop fitness for their sport if they seek to improve. All fitness tests assess, individually or in a combined manner, the 'S' factors, for example: speed strength; suppleness; strength; stamina. Skill being evaluated in specific tests as discussed. Fitness tests tend to be of two types, single or battery. Single tests, such as the vertical jump, measure one component. Batteries or groups of tests evaluate a range of 'S' factor qualities and therefore give the coach a broader picture of strengths and weaknesses.

The reality is that test batteries are made up of single tests! The coach has to identify which tests are more appropriate to the sport or the individual concerned. Indeed some, such as the standing long jump, can be tests of technical competence while in some activities being competitive events in their own right.

Governing bodies produce a range of tests to assess the fitness of participants. It is interesting to note that as technically distinct as sports may be, there is an uncanny similarity in their testing strategies. The components of fitness may be in a different mix for specific sports but the assessment of the components is similar if not identical.

Speed

1 SPRINTING Acceleration

Mark out with cones a start and finish line 15 m apart. The player stands with both feet behind the line. A sprint 'standing start' is best: one foot forward just behind the line, the other back. The easy way to time this activity is to allow the players to start in their own time and click the stopwatch as the rear foot (usually) breaks contact with the ground. The watch is stopped as the runner's torso crosses the line. Alternatively, use almost a sprint start triggered by the commands 'set, get ready, go' or a whistle blast.

* The activity can be repeated/modified using distances of between 5 and 30 metres or more as seems appropriate.

COACHING TIP

You can organise the test so that the player sprints along a pitch or marking line. This will spotlight the degree of balance and coordination and any wasted rotational movement. In most sports the acceleration phase is over a short distance. As the test distance lengthens, maintaining speed becomes an increasingly significant factor.

2 SPRINTING Maximum Speed/Speed Endurance

Mark out with cones a start and finish line 20 m apart. The player stands 10–20 m behind the start line and accelerates towards it, continuing to sprint flat out until he is past the finish line. The coach starts the watch as the player's torso crosses the start line and stops it when it has crossed the finish.

* The activity can be modified/repeated using distances of between 25 and 40 m or even longer if appropriate.

COACHING TIP

As with test 1, using a line to run on will indicate aspects of technique that need addressing. As the chosen distance lengthens the emphasis of the test will shift from maximum sprinting speed to speed endurance.

3 FAST FEET

Space 10 small cones or canes 45 cm apart, or use rope ladders, which are now available for these drills. The athlete runs with very short strides over the cones so that the feet hit the ground between them.

The activity can be repeated with both feet brought together between cones, the modified run can be led with left foot, the right foot, or alternate feet. A modified version is to stand sideways to the cones and run, leading with the left or right side.

COACHING TIP

Ensure that the athlete concentrates not just on foot speed but knee lift as well.

4 EXPLOSIVE LEG POWER

Use a wall and some chalk. Stand right side to the wall and chalk the fingers of the right hand. Reach as far up the wall as possible and make a mark with the tips of the fingers. When ready, squat slightly and jump as high as possible at the side of the wall reaching up with the extended right arm and hand making a chalk mark with the right hand. Measure the distance between the two marks. This gives an indication of the vertical height jumped.

*The activity can be repeated with the left side to the wall.

COACHING TIP
By testing a player on both sides the coach can evaluate a weakness which may need addressing.

5 STANDING LONG JUMP

Standing with both feet behind a line, the athlete gently swings both arms backwards to the fullest extent, then from this extreme range throws both arms forwards while at the same time jumping forwards, landing with both feet together. A sandpit, soft grass or a crash mat is recommended.

COACHING TIP

The activity can be repeated by taking off from the left or right foot. Wilf Paish's Jumping Decathlon (pages 119–29) is an excellent form of leg power assessment.

6 EXPLOSIVE ARM POWER

Standing with feet side by side behind a line the athlete holds a medicine ball in both hands close to the chest. The medicine ball is then pushed away in a 'chest pass' action as far as possible.

* The activity can be repeated using different actions and foot positions

COACHING TIP
Wilf Paish's Throwing Decathlon (pages 130–43) is an excellent form of arm power assessment and training.

7 HAMSTRING FLEXIBILITY

The athlete sits on the floor with the soles of both feet flat against the top of a bench. Keeping the legs straight, she or he reaches forwards with both arms extended as far as possible, and holds the position. Measure the distance from the bench top to the tips of the fingers.

COACHING TIP
Ensure that the legs are kept straight and there is no violent lunge forwards.

8 SHOULDER MOBILITY

The athlete stands with the feet shoulder-width apart, and lifts both arms to shoulder height with the palms facing forwards, then simultaneously pushes both arms gently backwards as far as possible and holds. Measure the distance between the backs of the hands.

COACHING TIP
Make certain that the athlete does not lean forwards and there is no jerking back of the arms.

9 LOWER BACK MOBILITY

The athlete lies on her or his front on the floor with a partner holding their ankles. The hands are placed at the side of the head and the chest lifted as far off the floor as possible, and held. Measure the distance from the floor to the shoulders and collar bone.

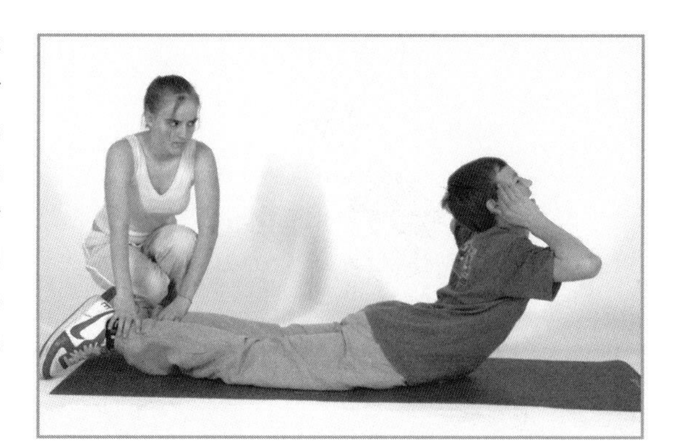

COACHING TIP

The partner must give a firm anchor for the legs. There should be no sudden movement.

10 FOUR × 10 M SHUTTLE RUNS

Mark out two lines 10 m apart. The athlete runs from one to the other placing one foot over the line before running back and doing the same again, and so on until four runs are completed. The activity can be repeated with 6 × 10, 8 × 10 or 10 × 10 runs.

COACHING TIP

The coach can select a distance according to the demands of the sport by modifying the distance between the lines and the number of runs. For the endurance-based athlete, Coachwise UK have produced a version of the shuttle run which operates between lines 20 m apart.

11 TIMED WALK/RUN

Using a running track or a measured distance of 600 m the athlete completes the distance as quickly as possible.

COACHING TIP

The coach can select a distance which is related to the demands of the sport or the position up to, say, 2000 m, or can specify a time, say, 2 minutes, and record the distance covered.

BATTERY TESTS

Apart from single tests there are, as discussed, those that embrace several activities. There are close similarities in the actual exercises used but the method of assessment varies. Two of the most popular tests used are Jumping and Throwing Decathlon, which measures aspects of leg and arm strength. Coaches may wish to use any number of the individual activities to assess particular aspects of fitness or all of them, which is a training session in its own right.

The tests listed in the following groupings have potential to assess performance in a wide variety of sports and can be used as training exercises in their own right. For example, the Overhead Throw can be used in soccer to assess a player's shoulder strength, in a skill-specific way, and monitor improvements. The coach can use the activity as a training exercise to improve strength and 'throw-in' distance.

The Jumping Decathlon

The first of the ten activities is the standing long jump, the second the standing triple jump. All the other activities are variations of hops, steps and jumps, the name describing the sequence of movements. 'Five spring jumps' are a series of five standing long jumps, one immediately following the other with no pause between. Most activities begin from a standing position except 'run, four hops and a jump', where a short run is allowed, and 'five stride long jump,' where a five-stride approach run is permitted. The '25-metre hop' is a timed event on the dominant or weaker leg. Other events are measured from the take-off line to the back of the heels on landing. If a student falls back on landing, too bad – measure to the nearest point of contact to the take off-line, hands or bottom.

1 STANDING LONG JUMP

Stand with feet shoulder-width apart, bend the knees and take both arms backwards. As you jump, throw both arms forwards and extend the legs. Bend the knees on landing.

2 STANDING TRIPLE JUMP

The old term 'hop, step and jump' is a much clearer way of describing this. Take off on the preferred (dominant) foot, land on the same foot, step onto the other foot and then take off into a jump, landing with both feet together.

3 TWO HOPS, STEP AND JUMP

Hop twice on one foot, step onto the other foot and then take off into a jump, landing with both feet together.

4 TWO HOPS, TWO STEPS AND JUMP

As above, but add an extra step before the jump.

5 TWO HOPS, TWO STEPS AND TWO JUMPS

As above, but add an extra jump.

6 FIVE SPRING JUMPS

Perform a series of five standing long jumps, one immediately following the other without pausing in between.

7 STANDING FOUR HOPS AND JUMP

From standing, perform four hops on one leg and then take off into a jump, landing with both feet together.

8 RUNNING FOUR HOPS AND JUMP

Take a short run-up, then perform four hops on one leg and then take off into a jump, landing with both feet together.

9 25-METRE HOP

This is a timed event on either the dominant or weaker leg.

10 FIVE-STRIDE LONG JUMP

Perform a five-stride run-up, then take off from one foot into a jump, landing with both feet together.

To work out the score, note the best of three attempts. Go down the appropriate column in table 8.1 to find the distance or time, or the nearest to it. Follow the line across to the left-hand side to give the score out of 100. I would suggest that you select three to five activities in a session, more than that is a training session in itself.

THE JUMPING DECATHLON — TABLE 8.1

	1 STAND LONG JUMP	2 STAND TRIPLE JUMP	3 2 HOPS, STEP & JUMP	4 2 HOPS, 2 STEPS & JUMP	5 2 HOPS, 2 STEPS 2 JUMPS	6 5 SPRING JUMPS	7 STAND 4 HOPS & JUMP	8 RUN 4 HOPS & JUMP	9 25-METRE HOP	10 5-STRIDE LONG JUMP
100	3.73	10.51	13.00	15.54	19.15	17.06	17.67	23.77	2.07	7.28
99	–	10.43	12.90	15.46	18.99	16.91	17.52	23.62	–	–
98	3.65	10.36	12.80	15.39	18.84	16.76	17.37	23.46	2.08	–
97	–	10.28	12.69	15.31	18.69	16.61	17.22	23.31	–	7.26
96	3.58	10.21	12.59	15.08	18.54	16.45	17.06	23.16	3.00	–
95	–	10.13	12.49	15.01	18.38	16.40	16.96	23.01	–	–
94	3.50	10.05	12.39	14.88	18.23	16.25	16.86	22.85	3.01	7.23
93	–	9.98	12.29	14.78	18.08	16.15	16.76	22.70	–	–
92	3.42	9.90	12.19	14.68	17.93	16.00	16.61	22.55	3.02	–
91	–	9.82	12.09	14.57	17.77	15.84	16.45	22.35	–	7.21
90	3.35	9.75	11.98	14.47	17.62	15.79	16.35	21.99	3.03	–
89	–	9.68	11.88	14.37	17.47	15.64	16.25	21.79	–	–
88	3.27	9.60	11.78	14.27	17.32	15.54	16.15	21.64	3.04	7.18
87	–	9.52	11.68	14.17	17.17	15.39	16.00	21.48	–	–
86	3.20	9.44	11.58	14.07	17.01	15.23	15.84	21.33	3.05	–
85	–	9.37	11.48	13.96	16.91	15.18	15.74	21.18	–	7.16

84	3.12	9.29	11.37	13.86	16.76	15.03	15.64	21.03	3.06	–
83	–	9.22	11.27	13.76	16.66	14.93	15.54	20.80	3.07	7.13
82	3.04	9.14	11.17	13.66	16.50	14.83	15.44	20.65	3.08	–
81	–	9.06	11.07	13.56	16.35	14.68	15.34	20.42	3.09	7.11
80	2.97	8.99	10.97	13.46	16.20	14.57	15.23	20.26	4.00	–
79	–	8.91	10.87	13.36	16.10	14.42	15.08	20.11	4.02	7.08
78	2.89	8.83	10.76	13.25	16.00	14.32	14.93	19.96	4.03	–
77	–	8.76	10.66	13.15	15.84	14.22	14.83	19.81	4.04	7.06
76	2.81	8.68	10.56	13.05	15.69	14.07	14.73	19.58	4.05	7.03
75	–	8.61	10.46	12.95	15.54	13.96	14.63	19.43	4.06	7.01
74	2.74	8.53	10.36	12.85	15.39	13.86	14.47	19.20	4.07	6.95
73	2.69	8.45	10.26	12.75	15.23	13.71	14.32	19.04	4.08	6.90
72	2.66	8.38	10.15	12.64	15.13	13.61	14.22	18.89	4.09	6.85
71	2.64	8.30	10.05	12.49	15.03	13.51	14.12	18.74	5.00	6.80
70	2.61	8.22	9.95	12.42	14.88	13.41	14.02	18.59	5.01	6.75
69	2.59	8.15	9.85	12.34	14.73	13.25	13.86	18.44	5.02	6.70
68	2.56	8.07	9.75	12.19	14.63	13.10	13.71	18.28	5.04	6.62
67	2.53	8.00	9.65	12.09	14.47	13.00	13.61	18.13	5.05	6.55
66	2.51	7.92	9.55	11.98	14.32	12.90	13.51	17.98	5.06	6.47
65	2.48	7.84	9.44	11.88	14.22	12.80	13.41	17.75	5.07	6.40
64	2.46	7.77	9.34	11.78	14.07	12.69	13.30	17.60	5.08	6.32

THE JUMPING DECATHLON cont

TABLE 8.1

	1 STAND LONG JUMP	2 STAND TRIPLE JUMP	3 2 HOPS, STEP & JUMP	4 2 HOPS, 2 STEPS & JUMP	5 2 HOPS, 2 STEPS 2 JUMPS	6 5 SPRING JUMPS	7 STAND 4 HOPS & JUMP	8 RUN 4 HOPS & JUMP	9 25-METRE HOP	10 5-STRIDE LONG JUMP
63	2.43	7.69	9.24	11.68	13.96	12.59	13.20	17.37	5.09	6.24
62	2.41	7.61	9.14	11.58	13.81	12.49	13.10	17.22	6.00	6.17
61	2.38	7.54	9.04	11.48	13.71	12.34	12.95	17.06	6.01	6.09
60	2.36	7.46	8.94	11.37	13.56	12.19	12.80	16.91	6.02	6.01
59	2.33	7.39	8.83	11.27	13.41	12.03	12.64	16.76	6.03	5.94
58	2.31	7.31	8.73	11.17	13.25	11.88	12.49	16.53	6.05	5.86
57	2.28	7.23	8.63	11.07	13.10	11.78	12.39	16.38	6.06	5.79
56	2.26	7.16	8.53	10.97	12.95	11.68	12.29	16.15	6.07	5.71
55	2.23	7.03	8.45	10.87	12.60	11.58	12.19	16.00	6.08	5.63
54	2.20	7.01	8.38	10.76	12.64	11.48	12.09	15.84	6.09	5.56
53	2.18	6.93	8.30	10.66	12.49	11.37	11.98	15.69	7.00	5.48
52	2.15	6.85	8.22	10.56	12.34	11.27	11.58	15.54	7.01	5.41
51	2.13	6.78	8.15	10.46	12.19	11.17	11.42	15.39	7.02	5.33
50	2.10	6.70	8.07	10.36	12.03	11.07	11.27	15.23	7.03	5.25
49	2.08	6.62	8.00	10.26	11.88	10.97	11.17	15.08	7.04	5.18
48	2.05	6.55	7.92	10.15	11.73	10.87	11.07	14.93	–	5.13

47	2.03	6.47	7.84	10.05	11.58	10.76	10.97	14.78	7.05	5.07
46	2.00	6.40	7.77	9.95	11.42	10.66	10.82	14.63	–	5.02
45	1.98	6.32	7.69	9.85	11.27	10.56	10.66	14.47	7.07	4.97
44	1.95	6.24	7.61	9.75	11.17	10.46	10.51	14.32	–	4.92
43	1.93	6.17	7.54	9.65	11.07	10.36	10.36	14.17	7.08	4.87
42	1.90	6.09	7.46	9.55	10.97	10.26	10.21	14.02	–	4.82
41	1.87	6.01	7.39	9.44	10.87	10.15	10.05	13.86	7.09	4.77
40	1.85	5.94	7.31	9.34	10.76	10.05	9.90	13.71	–	4.72
39	1.82	5.86	7.23	9.24	10.66	9.95	9.75	13.56	8.00	4.67
38	1.80	5.79	7.16	9.14	10.56	9.85	9.60	13.41	–	4.62
37	1.77	5.71	7.08	9.04	10.46	9.75	9.44	13.25	8.01	4.57
36	1.75	5.63	7.01	8.94	10.36	9.65	9.34	13.10	–	4.52
35	1.72	5.56	6.93	8.83	10.26	9.55	9.24	12.95	8.02	4.47
34	1.70	5.48	6.85	8.73	10.15	9.44	9.14	12.80	–	4.41
33	1.67	5.41	6.78	8.63	10.05	9.34	9.04	12.64	8.03	4.36
32	1.65	5.33	6.70	8.53	9.95	9.24	8.94	12.49	–	4.31
31	1.62	5.25	6.62	8.43	9.85	9.14	8.83	12.34	8.04	4.26
30	1.60	5.18	6.55	8.33	9.75	9.04	8.73	12.19	–	4.21
29	1.57	5.10	6.47	8.22	9.65	8.94	8.63	12.03	8.05	4.16
28	1.54	5.02	6.40	8.12	9.55	8.83	8.53	11.88	–	4.11
27	1.52	4.95	6.32	8.02	9.44	8.73	8.43	11.73	8.06	4.06

THE JUMPING DECATHLON cont — TABLE 8.1

	1 STAND LONG JUMP	2 STAND TRIPLE JUMP	3 2 HOPS, STEP & JUMP	4 2 HOPS, 2 STEPS & JUMP	5 2 HOPS, 2 STEPS 2 JUMPS	6 5 SPRING JUMPS	7 STAND 4 HOPS & JUMP	8 RUN 4 HOPS & JUMP	9 25-METRE HOP	10 5-STRIDE LONG JUMP
26	1.49	4.87	6.24	7.92	9.34	8.63	8.33	11.58	–	4.01
25	1.47	4.80	6.17	7.82	9.24	8.53	8.22	11.42	8.07	3.96
24	1.44	4.72	6.09	7.72	9.14	8.43	8.12	11.27	–	3.91
23	1.42	4.64	5.99	7.61	9.04	8.33	8.02	11.12	–	3.86
22	1.39	4.57	5.89	7.51	8.94	8.22	7.92	10.97	8.09	3.80
21	1.37	4.49	5.79	7.41	8.83	8.12	7.82	10.82	–	3.75
20	1.34	4.41	5.68	7.31	8.73	8.02	7.72	10.66	–	3.70
19	1.29	4.26	5.58	7.21	8.63	7.92	7.61	10.51	9.00	3.65
18	1.26	4.19	5.48	7.11	8.53	7.82	7.51	10.36	–	3.60
17	1.24	4.11	5.38	7.01	8.43	7.72	7.41	10.21	–	3.55
16	1.21	4.03	5.28	6.90	8.33	7.61	7.31	10.05	9.01	3.50
15	1.19	3.96	5.18	6.80	8.22	7.51	7.21	9.90	–	3.45
14	1.16	3.88	5.07	6.70	8.12	7.41	7.11	9.75	–	3.40
13	1.14	3.80	4.97	6.60	8.02	7.31	7.01	9.60	9.02	3.35
12	1.11	3.73	4.87	6.50	7.92	7.21	6.90	9.44	–	3.25
11	1.09	3.65	4.77	6.40	7.82	7.11	6.80	9.29	–	3.14

10	1.06	3.53	4.67	6.29	7.72	7.01	6.70	9.14	9.03	3.04
9	1.04	3.50	4.57	6.19	7.61	6.90	6.60	8.99	–	2.94
8	1.01	3.42	4.47	6.09	7.51	6.80	6.50	8.83	–	2.84
7	0.99	3.35	4.36	5.99	7.41	6.70	6.40	8.68	9.04	2.74
6	0.96	3.27	4.26	5.89	7.31	6.60	6.29	8.53	–	2.64
5	0.93	3.20	4.16	5.79	7.21	6.50	6.19	8.38	–	2.53
4	0.91	3.12	4.06	5.68	7.11	6.40	6.09	8.22	9.05	2.43
3	0.88	3.04	3.96	5.58	7.01	6.29	5.99	8.07	–	2.33
2	0.86	2.97	3.86	5.48	6.90	6.19	5.89	7.92	–	2.23
1	0.60	2.89	3.75	5.38	6.70	6.09	5.79	7.77	9.06	2.13

The Throwing Decathlon

Throw from behind a suitable line or mark and measure to the point where the medicine ball, or similar, lands. Scoring (table 8.2) is as for the Jumping Decathlon.

1 OVERHEAD DOUBLE-HANDED THROW

Hold a medicine ball in both hands facing away from the direction of the throw. Lift the medicine ball upwards and over the head while quickly straightening the legs. Continue the backward movement of the arm and let go of the ball over and behind the head.

2 KNEELING PUTT – DOMINANT ARM

Hold the medicine ball in the right hand under the right ear. Turn the shoulders away from the direction of the throw. Then drive the right shoulder round and forwards, finally pushing the medicine ball away from the body. This description presumes that the athlete is right-handed. If the athlete is left-handed, simply transpose the knee, hand and throwing position.

3 THROW THROUGH LEGS

Put both arms behind the legs and hold the medicine ball in both hands. With a flick of the wrist, throw the medicine ball upwards and forwards.

4 STANDING DISCUS THROW

With a right-handed athlete, the left foot should be forwards and the right foot back, and vice versa for left-handers. Turn the body as far as possible away from the direction of the throw. Drive the hips forwards, followed by the trunk and arms. Release the medicine ball with a final fling of the arm.

5 HAMMER-STYLE THROW

Turn the back away from the direction of the throw, holding the medicine ball in both hands as far over to the left side as possible (if the athlete is left-handed, they should start with the ball on the right-hand side). Drive the right hip, trunk and arms forwards. Lift the arms to deliver the medicine ball high over the left side (or right side for left handers).

6 FOOTBALL-STYLE THROW-IN

Right-handed throwers should start with their left foot forward, left handers with their right foot forward. Lean back as far as possible, holding the medicine ball in both hands. Drive the right hip, trunk and arms forwards and release the medicine ball over the left foot (left hip and right foot respectively for left handers).

7 PUSH FROM CHEST

Facing in the direction of the throw, hold the medicine ball in both hands at chest height, elbows high. Vigorously extend the arms to release the ball with a final flick of the wrists.

8 CABER THROW

Facing in the direction of the throw, hold the medicine ball in both hands between the knees. Drive the legs, hips and arms upwards and forwards to release the ball.

9 KNEELING PUTT – NON-DOMINANT ARM

See 'Kneeling putt – dominant arm' but perform with the weaker arm – i.e. right handers will use the left arm and left-handers the right arm.

10 BACK LYING OVERHEAD THROW

Lying on the back with the head towards the direction of the throw, hold the medicine ball in both hands, resting it on the legs. Drive the arms upwards towards the direction of the throw, releasing the medicine ball over the head.

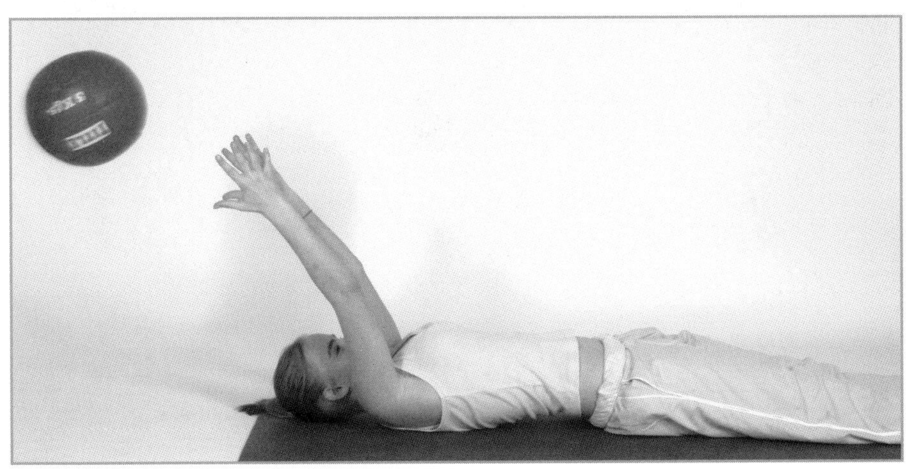

THE THROWING DECATHLON — TABLE 8.2

	1 OVERHEAD DOUBLE-HANDED THROW	2 KNEELING PUTT DOMINANT ARM	3 THROW THROUGH LEGS	4 STANDING DISCUS THROW	5 HAMMMER-STYLE THROW	6 FOOTBALL-STYLE THROW-IN	7 PUSH FROM CHEST	8 CABER THROW	9 KNEELING PUTT NON-DOMINANT ARM	10 BACK LYING OVERHEAD THROW
100	22.00	14.00	6.00	30.00	30.00	20.00	20.00	25.00	12.00	10.00
99	21.78	13.86	5.94	29.70	29.70	19.80	19.80	24.75	11.88	9.90
98	21.56	13.72	5.88	29.40	29.40	19.60	19.60	24.50	11.76	9.80
97	21.34	13.58	5.82	29.10	29.10	19.40	19.40	24.25	11.64	9.70
96	21.12	13.44	5.76	28.80	28.80	19.20	19.20	24.00	11.52	9.60
95	20.90	13.30	5.70	28.50	28.50	19.00	19.00	23.75	11.40	9.50
94	20.68	13.16	5.64	28.20	28.20	18.80	18.80	23.50	11.28	9.40
93	20.46	13.02	5.58	27.90	27.90	18.60	18.60	23.25	11.16	9.30
92	20.24	12.88	5.52	27.60	27.60	18.40	18.40	23.00	11.04	9.20
91	20.02	12.74	5.46	27.30	27.30	18.20	18.20	22.75	10.92	9.10
90	19.80	12.60	5.40	27.00	27.00	18.00	18.00	22.50	10.80	9.00
89	19.58	12.46	5.34	26.70	26.70	17.80	17.80	22.25	10.68	8.90
88	19.36	12.32	5.28	26.40	26.40	17.60	17.60	22.00	10.56	8.80
87	19.14	12.18	5.22	26.10	26.10	17.40	17.40	21.75	10.44	8.70
86	18.92	12.04	5.16	25.80	25.80	17.20	17.20	21.50	10.32	8.60
85	18.70	11.90	5.10	25.50	25.50	17.00	17.00	21.25	10.20	8.50

84	18.48	11.76	5.04	25.20	25.20	16.80	16.80	21.00	10.00	8.40
83	18.26	11.62	4.98	24.90	24.90	16.60	16.60	20.75	9.96	8.30
82	18.04	11.48	4.92	24.60	24.60	16.40	16.40	20.50	9.84	8.20
81	17.82	11.34	4.86	24.30	24.30	16.20	16.20	20.25	9.72	8.10
80	17.60	11.20	4.80	24.00	24.00	16.00	16.00	20.00	9.60	8.00
79	17.38	11.06	4.74	23.70	23.70	15.80	15.80	19.75	9.48	7.90
78	17.16	10.92	4.68	23.40	23.40	15.60	15.60	19.50	9.36	7.80
77	16.94	10.78	4.62	23.10	23.10	15.40	15.40	19.25	9.24	7.70
76	16.72	10.64	4.56	22.80	22.80	15.20	15.20	19.00	9.12	7.60
75	16.50	10.50	4.50	22.50	22.50	15.00	15.00	18.75	9.00	7.50
74	16.28	10.36	4.44	22.20	22.20	14.80	14.80	18.50	8.88	7.40
73	16.06	10.22	4.38	21.90	21.90	14.60	14.60	18.25	8.76	7.30
72	15.84	10.08	4.32	21.60	21.60	14.40	14.40	18.00	8.64	7.20
71	15.62	9.94	4.25	21.30	21.30	14.20	14.20	17.75	8.52	7.10
70	15.40	9.80	4.20	21.00	21.00	14.00	14.00	17.50	8.40	7.00
69	15.18	9.66	4.14	20.70	20.70	13.80	13.80	17.25	8.28	6.90
68	14.96	9.52	4.08	20.40	20.40	13.60	13.60	17.00	8.16	6.80
67	14.74	9.38	4.02	20.10	20.10	13.40	13.40	16.75	8.04	6.70
66	14.52	9.24	3.96	19.80	19.80	13.20	13.20	16.50	7.92	6.60
65	14.30	9.10	3.90	19.50	19.50	13.00	13.00	16.25	7.80	6.50
64	14.08	8.96	3.84	19.20	19.20	12.80	12.80	16.00	7.68	6.40

THE THROWING DECATHLON cont

TABLE 8.2

	1 OVERHEAD DOUBLE-HANDED THROW	2 KNEELING PUTT DOMINANT ARM	3 THROW THROUGH LEGS	4 STANDING DISCUS THROW	5 HAMMMER-STYLE THROW	6 FOOTBALL-STYLE THROW-IN	7 PUSH FROM CHEST	8 CABER THROW	9 KNEELING PUTT NON-DOMINANT ARM	10 BACK LYING OVERHEAD THROW
63	13.86	8.82	3.78	18.90	18.90	12.60	12.60	15.75	7.56	6.30
62	13.64	8.68	3.72	18.60	18.60	12.40	12.40	15.50	7.44	6.20
61	13.42	8.54	3.66	18.30	18.30	12.20	12.20	15.25	7.32	6.10
60	13.20	8.40	3.60	18.00	18.00	12.00	12.00	15.00	7.20	6.00
59	12.98	8.26	3.54	17.70	17.70	11.80	11.80	14.75	7.08	5.90
58	12.76	8.12	3.48	17.40	17.40	11.60	11.60	14.50	6.96	5.80
57	12.54	7.98	3.42	17.10	17.10	11.40	11.40	14.25	6.84	5.70
56	12.32	7.84	3.36	16.80	16.80	11.20	11.20	14.00	6.72	5.60
55	12.10	7.70	3.30	16.50	16.50	11.00	11.00	13.75	6.60	5.50
54	11.88	7.56	3.24	16.20	16.20	10.80	10.80	13.50	6.48	5.40
53	11.66	7.42	3.18	15.90	15.90	10.60	10.60	13.25	6.36	5.30
52	11.44	7.28	3.12	15.60	15.60	10.40	10.40	13.00	6.24	5.20
51	11.22	7.14	3.06	15.30	15.30	10.20	10.20	12.75	6.12	5.10
50	11.00	7.00	3.00	15.00	15.00	10.00	10.00	12.50	6.00	5.00
49	10.78	6.86	2.94	14.70	14.70	9.80	9.80	12.25	5.88	4.90
48	10.56	6.72	2.88	14.40	14.40	9.60	9.60	12.00	5.76	4.80

47	10.34	6.58	2.82	14.10	14.10	9.40	9.40	11.75	5.64	4.70
46	10.12	6.44	2.76	13.80	13.80	9.20	9.20	11.50	5.52	4.60
45	9.90	6.30	2.70	13.50	13.50	9.00	9.00	11.25	5.40	4.50
44	9.68	6.16	2.64	13.20	13.20	8.80	8.80	11.00	5.28	4.40
43	9.46	6.02	2.58	12.90	12.90	8.60	8.60	10.75	5.16	4.30
42	9.24	5.88	2.52	12.60	12.60	8.40	8.40	10.50	5.04	4.20
41	9.02	5.74	2.46	12.30	12.30	8.20	8.20	10.25	4.92	4.10
40	8.80	5.60	2.40	12.00	12.00	8.00	8.00	10.00	4.80	4.00
39	8.58	5.46	2.34	11.70	11.70	7.80	7.80	9.75	4.68	3.90
38	8.36	5.32	2.28	11.40	11.40	7.60	7.60	9.50	4.56	3.80
37	8.14	5.18	2.22	11.10	11.10	7.40	7.40	9.25	4.48	3.70
36	7.92	5.04	2.16	10.80	10.80	7.20	7.20	9.00	4.32	3.60
35	7.70	4.90	2.10	10.50	10.50	7.00	7.00	8.75	4.20	3.50
34	7.48	4.76	2.04	10.20	10.20	6.80	6.80	8.50	4.08	3.40
33	7.26	4.62	1.98	9.90	9.90	6.60	6.60	8.25	3.96	3.30
32	7.04	4.48	1.92	9.60	9.60	6.40	6.40	8.00	3.84	3.20
31	6.82	4.34	1.86	9.30	9.30	6.20	6.20	7.75	3.72	3.10
30	6.60	4.20	1.80	9.00	9.00	6.00	6.00	7.50	3.60	3.00
29	6.38	4.06	1.74	8.70	8.70	5.80	5.80	7.25	3.48	2.90
28	6.16	3.92	1.68	8.40	8.40	5.60	5.60	7.00	3.36	2.80
27	5.94	3.78	1.62	8.10	8.10	5.40	5.40	6.75	3.24	2.70

THE THROWING DECATHLON cont

TABLE 8.2

	1 OVERHEAD DOUBLE-HANDED THROW	2 KNEELING PUTT DOMINANT ARM	3 THROW THROUGH LEGS	4 STANDING DISCUS THROW	5 HAMMMER-STYLE THROW	6 FOOTBALL-STYLE THROW-IN	7 PUSH FROM CHEST	8 CABER THROW	9 KNEELING PUTT NON-DOMINANT ARM	10 BACK LYING OVERHEAD THROW
26	5.72	3.64	1.56	7.80	7.80	5.20	5.20	6.50	3.12	2.60
25	5.50	3.50	1.50	7.50	7.50	5.00	5.00	6.25	3.00	2.50
24	5.28	3.36	1.44	7.20	7.20	4.80	4.80	6.00	2.88	2.40
23	5.06	3.22	1.38	6.90	6.90	4.60	4.60	5.75	2.76	2.30
22	4.84	3.08	1.32	6.60	6.60	4.40	4.40	5.50	2.64	2.20
21	4.62	2.94	1.26	6.30	6.30	4.20	4.20	5.25	2.52	2.10
20	4.40	2.80	1.20	6.00	6.00	4.00	4.00	5.00	2.40	2.00
19	4.18	2.66	1.14	5.70	5.70	3.80	3.80	4.75	2.28	1.90
18	3.96	2.52	1.08	5.40	5.40	3.60	3.60	4.50	2.16	1.80
17	3.74	2.38	1.02	5.10	5.10	3.40	3.40	4.25	2.04	1.70
16	3.52	2.24	0.96	4.80	4.80	3.20	3.20	4.00	1.92	1.60
15	3.30	2.10	0.90	4.50	4.50	3.00	3.00	3.75	1.80	1.50
14	3.08	1.96	0.84	4.20	4.20	2.80	2.80	3.50	1.68	1.40
13	2.86	1.82	0.78	3.90	3.90	2.60	2.60	3.25	1.56	1.30
12	2.64	1.68	0.72	3.60	3.60	2.40	2.40	3.00	1.44	1.20
11	2.42	1.54	0.66	3.30	3.30	2.20	2.20	2.75	1.32	1.10

10	2.20	1.40	0.60	3.00	3.00	2.00	2.00	2.50	1.20	1.00
9	1.98	1.26	0.54	2.70	2.70	1.80	1.80	2.25	1.08	0.90
8	1.76	1.12	0.48	2.40	2.40	1.60	1.60	2.00	0.96	0.80
7	1.54	0.98	0.42	2.10	2.10	1.40	1.40	1.75	0.84	0.70
6	1.32	0.84	0.36	1.80	1.80	1.20	1.20	1.50	0.72	0.60
5	1.10	0.70	0.30	1.50	1.50	1.00	1.00	1.25	0.60	0.50
4	0.88	0.56	0.24	1.20	1.20	0.80	0.80	1.00	0.48	0.40
3	0.66	0.42	0.18	0.90	0.90	0.60	0.60	0.75	0.36	0.30
2	0.44	0.28	0.12	0.60	0.60	0.40	0.40	0.50	0.24	0.20
1	0.22	0.14	0.06	0.30	0.30	0.20	0.20	0.25	0.12	0.10
0	0.00	0.00	0.00	0.00	0.00	0.00	0.00	0.00	0.00	0.00

The Fitness Decathlon

Having found both these tests most useful both as diagnostic and training activies I developed a test battery of my own – the Fitness Decathlon! Mine differs slightly in that it was devised to measure strength, speed, suppleness and stamina in a variety of sport-specific ways. Scoring is as the other 'Decathlons' (table 8.3). I have used and modified recognised tests of fitness and made them much more user-friendly. In a general coaching 'how to' manual such as this it is not possible to discuss the physiology and diagnostic potential of these tests. I would suggest that coaches accept them on the face of it for what they are. The only major difference in the nature of this battery is that in two tests I have had to allow for variations in heart rate between the sexes.

1 VERTICAL JUMP

Standing next to a wall, reach as far up the wall as possible and make a mark using chalk. Squat down, then jump up vertically, and make a mark at the highest part of the jump. Measure the distance between the marks.

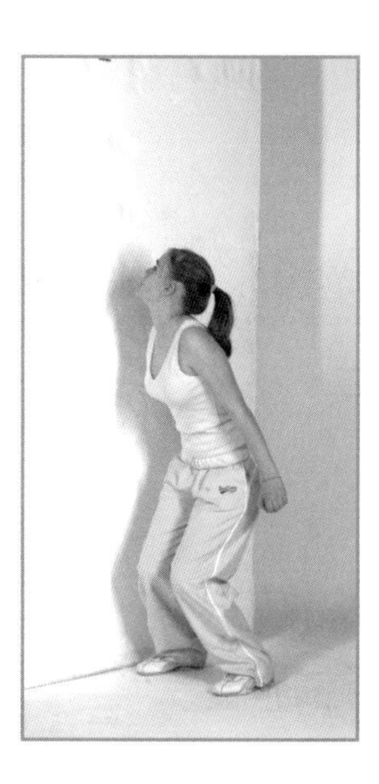

2 4 × 10-METRE SHUTTLE RUN

At the start of the shuttle run, the front foot is behind the line. The two lines are 10 m apart, and at each turn one foot is required to be placed over the line. Perform four runs.

3 10 × 10-METRE SHUTTLE RUN

As above, but perform ten runs.

4 SIT-UPS

The knees should be bent to 90 degrees with the hands at the side of the head and feet flat on the floor, shoulder-width apart. For comfort and safety, use a mat or similar soft surface. Count the number performed in one minute.

5 PRESS-UPS

The legs, back and shoulders must be in a straight line throughout the movement. Count the number performed in one minute.

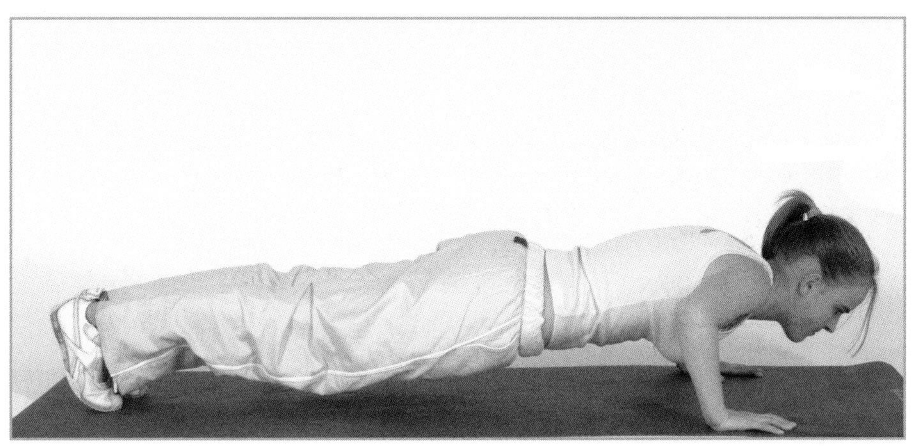

6 3-MINUTE STEP TEST

Stand close to a gym bench with the feet side by side. The bench should be about 30 cm high. The rhythm is right foot on, left foot on, right foot off, left foot off and so on. The rate of stepping is 25 per minute (a metronome is useful, but the rate is soon learned). Take a pulse count for one minute immediately on finishing the test. Note the different scoring system for men and women in table 8.3.

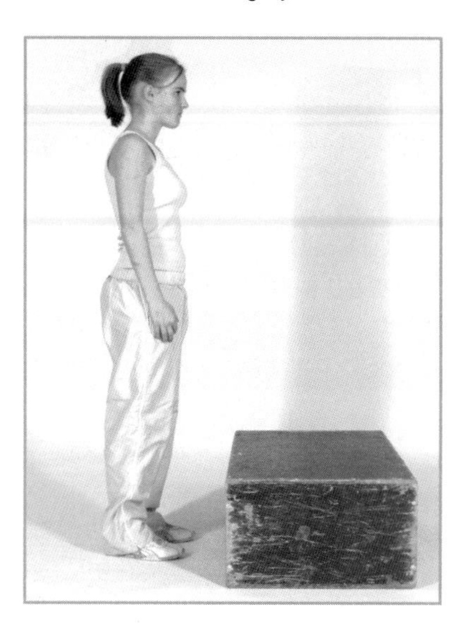

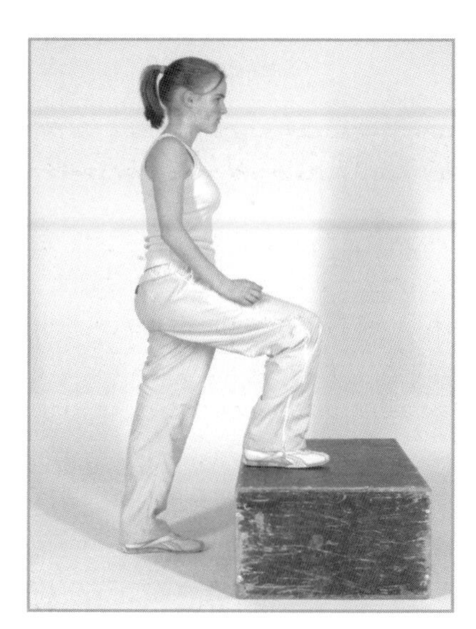

7 5-MINUTE STEP TEST

Follow the same rhythm as above, but perform 30 steps a minute. Take a pulse count for one minute one minute after finishing. The reasoning behind the different tests is simply that the three-minute test assesses heart rate response to exercise and the five-minute test measures rate of recovery. Note the different scoring system for men and women in table 8.3.

8 HAMSTRING FLEXIBILITY

Sit on the floor with the legs straight and the feet touching the top of a bench, which should be laid on its side. Reach as far forwards as possible and hold for three seconds. Measure the distance between the bench top to the furthest point reached. Note that in table 8.3, distances beyond the bench top are marked + and distances not as far as the bench top are marked –.

9 HIP MOBILITY TEST

Sit on the floor and spread the legs as wide as possible. Place a hinged DIY rule along the inside of each leg. Use a protractor to measure the angle.

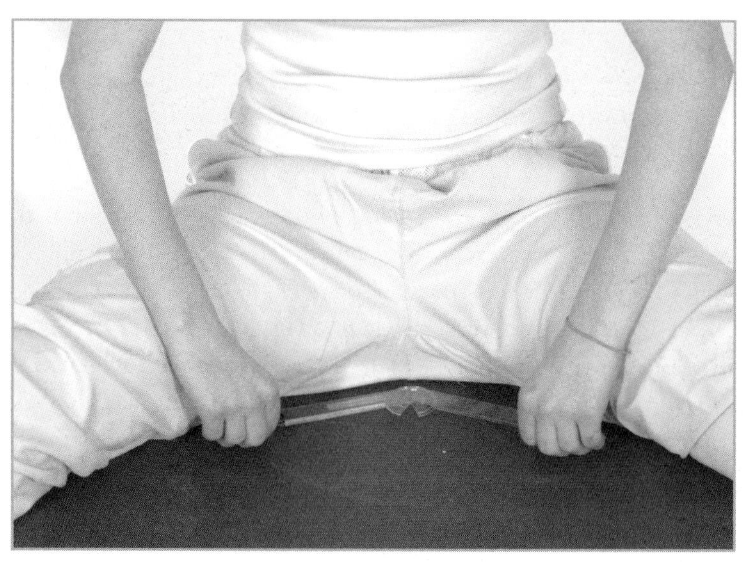

10 TURN AND REACH TEST

Make a vertical mark on a wall. Stand left-side on with the feet in line with the mark. Reach around with the right arm to touch the wall and measure the distance. Note that in table 8.3, distances beyond the line are marked + and distances not as far as the line are marked –.

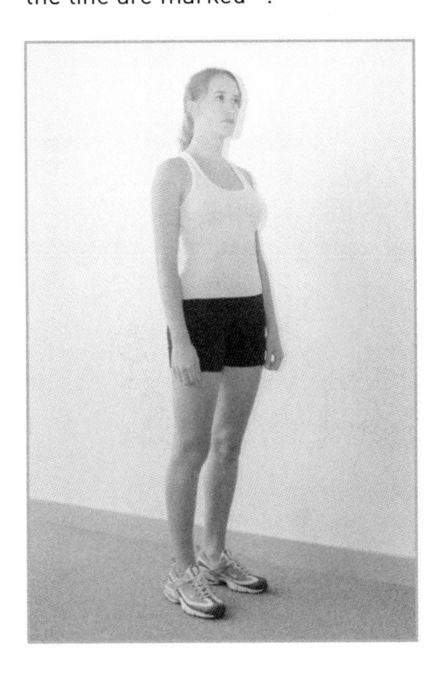

The examples presented give only a glimpse of the tens of thousands that exist. Most are generic in their application but some are sport-specific. However, someone at some time devised them! They were ordinary coaches and teachers just like you. The ones that work have stood the test of time and have become part of the general repertoire. With a little imagination we can all devise a method of testing a particular skill or aspect of fitness that is appropriate to the situation and the individuals involved. Sometimes the answer might be to adapt an existing test and make it more user-friendly. Interestingly, most tests were devised for adults and might not reflect too well the competence of an aspiring youngster. Only the coach can identify the specific needs of a player and just what needs evaluating and the best method of doing so. Tests and measures can be a most useful tool in the coaching armoury and can be vital in ensuring the continued improvement of the young performer.

THE FITNESS DECATHLON

TABLE 8.3

	1 VERTICAL JUMP	2 4 × 10 m SHUTTLE RUN	3 10 × 10 m SHUTTLE RUN	4 SIT-UPS	5 PRESS-UPS	6 3-MINUTE STEP TEST		7 5-MINUTE STEP TEST		8 HAMSTRING FLEXIBILITY TEST	9 HIP MOBILITY TEST	10 TURN AND REACH TEST
						F	M	F	M			
100	1.00	8.00	20.00	80	80	100	110	70	80	+25.0	180.0	+1.00
99	0.99	8.05	20.10	79	79	101	111	71	81	+24.5	178.5	+0.98
98	0.98	8.10	20.20	78	78	102	112	72	82	+24.0	177.0	+0.96
97	0.97	8.15	20.30	77	77	103	113	73	83	+23.5	175.5	+0.94
96	0.96	8.20	20.40	76	76	104	114	74	84	+23.0	174.0	+0.92
95	0.95	8.25	20.50	75	75	105	115	75	85	+22.5	172.5	+0.90
94	0.94	8.30	20.60	74	74	106	116	76	86	+22.0	171.0	+0.88
93	0.93	8.35	20.70	73	73	107	117	77	87	+21.5	169.5	+0.86
92	0.92	8.40	20.80	72	72	108	118	78	88	+21.0	168.0	+0.84
91	0.91	8.45	20.90	71	71	109	119	79	89	+20.5	166.5	+0.82
90	0.90	8.50	21.00	70	70	110	120	80	90	+20.0	165.0	+0.80
89	0.89	8.55	21.10	69	69	111	121	81	91	+19.5	163.5	+0.78
88	0.88	8.60	21.20	68	68	112	122	82	92	+19.0	162.0	+0.76
87	0.87	8.65	21.30	67	67	113	123	83	93	+18.5	160.5	+0.74
86	0.86	8.70	21.40	66	66	114	124	84	94	+18.0	159.0	+0.72
85	0.85	8.75	21.50	65	65	115	125	85	95	+17.5	157.5	+0.70
84	0.84	8.80	21.60	64	64	116	126	86	96	+17.0	156.0	+0.68

83	0.83	8.85	21.70	63	63	117	127	87	97	+16.5	154.5	+0.66
82	0.82	8.90	21.80	62	62	118	128	88	98	+16.0	153.0	+0.64
81	0.81	8.95	21.90	61	61	119	129	89	99	+15.5	151.5	+0.62
80	0.80	9.00	22.00	60	60	120	130	90	100	+15.0	150.0	+0.60
79	0.79	9.05	22.10	59	59	121	131	91	101	+14.5	148.5	+0.58
78	0.78	9.10	22.20	58	58	122	132	92	102	+14.0	147.0	+0.56
77	0.77	9.15	22.30	57	57	123	133	93	103	+13.5	145.5	+0.54
76	0.76	9.20	22.40	56	56	124	134	94	104	+13.0	144.0	+0.52
75	0.75	9.25	22.50	55	55	125	135	95	105	+12.5	142.5	+0.50
74	0.74	9.30	22.60	54	54	126	136	96	106	+12.0	141.0	+0.48
73	0.73	9.35	22.70	53	53	127	137	97	107	+11.5	139.5	+0.46
72	0.72	9.40	22.80	52	52	128	138	98	108	+11.0	138.0	+0.44
71	0.71	9.45	22.90	51	51	129	139	99	109	+10.5	136.5	+0.42
70	0.70	9.50	23.00	50	50	130	140	100	110	+10.0	135.0	+0.40
69	0.69	9.55	23.15	49	49	131	141	101	111	+9.5	133.5	+0.38
68	0.68	9.60	23.30	48	48	132	142	102	112	+9.0	132.0	+0.36
67	0.67	9.65	23.45	47	47	133	143	103	113	+8.5	130.5	+0.34
66	0.66	9.70	23.60	46	46	134	144	104	114	+8.0	129.0	+0.32
65	0.65	9.75	23.75	45	45	135	145	105	115	+7.5	127.5	+0.30
64	0.64	9.80	23.90	44	44	136	146	106	116	+7.0	126.0	+0.28
63	0.63	9.85	24.00	43	43	137	147	107	117	+6.5	124.5	+0.26

THE FITNESS DECATHLON — TABLE 8.3

	1 VERTICAL JUMP	2 4 × 10 m SHUTTLE RUN	3 10 × 10 m SHUTTLE RUN	4 SIT-UPS	5 PRESS-UPS	6 3-MINUTE STEP TEST		7 5-MINUTE STEP TEST		8 HAMSTRING FLEXIBILITY TEST	9 HIP MOBILITY TEST	10 TURN AND REACH TEST
						F	M	F	M			
62	0.62	9.90	24.15	42	42	138	148	108	118	+6.0	123.0	+0.24
61	0.61	9.95	24.30	41	41	139	149	109	119	+5.5	121.5	+0.22
60	0.60	10.00	24.45	40	40	140	150	110	120	+5.0	120.0	+0.20
59	0.59	10.05	24.60	39	39	141	151	111	121	+4.5	118.5	+0.18
58	0.58	10.10	24.75	38	38	142	152	112	122	+4.0	117.0	+0.16
57	0.57	10.15	24.90	37	37	143	153	113	123	+3.5	115.5	+0.14
56	0.56	10.20	25.00	36	36	144	154	114	124	+3.0	114.0	+0.12
55	0.55	10.25	25.15	35	35	145	155	115	125	+2.5	112.5	+0.10
54	0.54	10.30	25.30	34	34	146	156	116	126	+2.0	111.0	+0.08
53	0.53	10.35	25.45	33	33	147	157	117	127	+1.5	109.5	+0.06
52	0.52	10.40	25.60	32	32	148	158	118	128	+1.0	108.0	+0.04
51	0.51	10.45	25.75	31	31	149	159	119	129	+0.5	106.5	+0.02
50	0.50	10.50	25.90	30	30	150	160	120	130	0.0	105.0	0.00
49	0.49	10.55	26.00	29	29	151	161	121	131	–0.5	103.5	–0.02
48	0.48	10.60	26.15	28	28	152	162	122	132	–1.0	102.0	–0.04
47	0.47	10.65	26.30	27	27	153	163	123	133	–1.5	100.5	–0.06
46	0.46	10.70	26.45	26	26	154	164	124	134	–2.0	99.0	–0.08

45	0.45	10.75	26.60	25	25	155	165	125	135	−2.5	97.5	−0.10
44	0.44	10.80	26.75	24	24	156	166	126	136	−3.0	96.0	−0.12
43	0.43	10.85	26.90	23	23	157	167	127	137	−3.5	94.5	−0.14
42	0.42	10.90	27.00	22	22	158	168	128	138	−4.0	93.0	−0.16
41	0.41	10.95	27.15	21	21	159	169	129	139	−4.5	91.5	−0.18
40	0.40	11.00	27.30	20	20	160	170	130	140	−5.0	90.0	−0.20
39	0.39	11.05	27.45	–	–	161	171	131	141	−5.5	88.5	−0.22
38	0.38	11.10	27.60	19	19	162	172	132	142	−6.0	87.0	−0.24
37	0.37	11.15	27.75	–	–	163	173	133	143	−6.5	85.5	−0.26
36	0.36	11.20	27.90	18	18	164	174	134	144	−7.0	84.0	−0.28
35	0.35	11.25	28.00	–	–	165	175	135	145	−7.5	82.5	−0.30
34	0.34	11.30	28.15	17	17	166	176	136	146	−8.0	81.0	−0.32
33	0.33	11.35	28.30	–	–	167	177	137	147	−8.5	79.5	−0.34
32	0.32	11.40	28.45	16	16	168	178	138	148	−9.0	78.0	−0.36
31	0.31	11.45	28.60	–	–	169	179	139	149	−9.5	76.5	−0.38
30	0.30	11.50	28.75	15	15	170	180	140	150	−10.0	75.0	−0.40
29	0.29	11.55	29.00	–	–	171	181	141	151	−10.5	73.5	−0.42
28	0.28	11.60	29.15	14	14	172	182	142	152	−11.0	72.0	−0.44
27	0.27	11.65	29.30	–	–	173	183	143	153	−11.5	70.5	−0.46
26	0.26	11.70	29.45	13	13	174	184	144	154	−12.0	69.0	−0.48
25	0.25	11.75	29.60	–	–	175	185	145	155	−12.5	67.5	−0.50

THE FITNESS DECATHLON TABLE 8.3

	1 VERTICAL JUMP	2 4 × 10 m SHUTTLE RUN	3 10 × 10 m SHUTTLE RUN	4 SIT-UPS	5 PRESS-UPS	6 3-MINUTE STEP TEST		7 5-MINUTE STEP TEST		8 HAMSTRING FLEXIBILITY TEST	9 HIP MOBILITY TEST	10 TURN AND REACH TEST
						F	M	F	M			
24	0.24	11.80	29.75	12	12	176	186	146	156	−13.0	66.0	−0.52
23	0.23	11.85	29.90	–	–	177	187	147	157	−13.5	64.5	−0.54
22	0.22	11.90	30.00	11	11	178	188	148	158	−14.0	63.0	−0.56
21	0.21	11.95	30.15	–	–	179	189	149	159	−14.5	61.5	−0.58
20	0.20	12.00	30.30	10	10	180	190	150	160	−15.0	60.0	−0.60
19	0.19	12.05	30.45	–	–	181	191	151	161	−15.5	58.5	−0.62
18	0.18	12.10	30.60	9	9	182	192	152	162	−16.0	57.0	−0.64
17	0.17	12.15	30.75	–	–	183	193	153	163	−16.5	55.5	−0.66
16	0.16	12.20	30.90	8	8	184	194	154	164	−17.0	54.0	−0.68
15	0.15	12.25	31.00	–	–	185	195	155	165	−17.5	52.5	−0.70
14	0.14	12.30	31.15	7	7	186	196	156	166	−18.0	51.0	−0.72
13	0.13	12.35	31.30	–	–	187	197	157	167	−18.5	49.5	−0.74
12	0.12	12.40	31.45	6	6	188	198	158	168	−19.0	48.0	−0.76
11	0.11	12.45	31.60	–	–	189	199	159	169	−19.5	46.5	−0.78
10	0.10	12.50	31.75	5	5	190	200	160	170	−20.0	45.0	−0.80
9	0.09	12.55	31.90	–	–	191	201	161	171	−20.5	43.5	−0.82
8	0.08	12.60	32.00	4	4	192	202	162	172	−21.0	42.0	−0.84

7	0.07	12.65	32.15	–	–	193	203	163	173	–21.5	40.5	–0.86
6	0.06	12.70	32.30	3	3	194	204	164	174	–22.0	39.0	–0.88
5	0.05	12.75	32.45	–	–	195	205	165	175	–22.5	37.5	–0.90
4	0.04	12.80	32.60	2	2	196	206	166	176	–23.0	36.0	–0.92
3	0.03	12.85	32.75	–	–	197	207	167	177	–23.5	34.5	–0.94
2	0.02	12.90	32.90	1	1	198	208	168	178	–24.0	33.0	–0.96
1	0.01	12.95	33.00	–	–	199	209	169	179	–24.5	31.5	–0.98
0	0.00	13.00	33.15	–	–	200	210	170	180	–25.0	30.0	–1.00

CHAPTER 9 TRAINING SCHEDULES

I have detailed the theory behind the planning of training schedules that takes into account the skill and fitness requirements of the sport. However, despite the fact that 'training theory' and the 'periodisation of training' are now accepted concepts in the sporting world, the degree to which they are applied differs considerably. This variation occurs naturally between sports since they have specific needs that can be quite different. Surprisingly, however, variations do occur within the sport itself. The aim of this section is to present examples of training sessions for a variety of sports to give a feeling of both the structure and the manner in which theories can be applied in practice.

The training year is generally subdivided into:

Preparation

- active recovery – recreational participation post/pre-season
- pre-season – general strength and endurance – establishing basic skills.

Competition

- early season – gross strength and endurance – refinement of skills
- mid-season – speed and power – technical and tactical focus
- end of season – major fixtures? Peak performance.

I have presented a synopsis of training identifying the emphasis of work in a given week, pre-, early and end of season, to show the subtle developments in the training loads. The programmes are aimed at the post-pubertal to post-18 age groups. Days are presented merely as an indicator of the focus of activity in a given session; in some cases, as with rowing and athletics, some specific details are given, with others generic structures are presented. It is for the coach to prescribe the content of a session since it needs to be very specific to the needs of each and every participant. Some may require less, others more. The examples given are merely that, an insight into the process; they are not meant to be applied to all players.

There are with most training programmes elements which are sport-specific and therefore are the domain of the technical and tactical authority, the coach. Similarly with those elements that are designated strength and related activity. I have written extensively on weight, resistance, circuit and other strength-related activities. It is not in the scope of this book to go into the detail of specific regimes. However, there is an issue that does need to be addressed regarding this topic.

It is generally accepted that weight training should not form part of the programme for a young athlete. Musculo-skeletal development during the period up to and beyond puberty is not conducive to heavy loadings on joints generally and the vertebral column in particular. Sustained intensive loadings and those that can occur with some 'explosive' drills are also contraindicated. This does not mean that strength training cannot be included in a schedule. The general consensus of opinion is that athletes should use only their own bodyweight in the pre-pubertal period. From 14 to 16 years weight training using light loads may be introduced at the coach's discretion. From 16 onwards loadings can be increased towards maximal at 18 years and above.

The use of 'free weights' must only take place under qualified supervision. On no account should youngsters be allowed to train on their own. Coaches should ensure that safety in the training area is a priority and that safe techniques are taught. Using multi-gym equipment can make training with weights far safer. However, youngsters can get carried away with the environment and attempt loads that are beyond their ability. Supervision at all times is required.

Strength training in one form or another is an essential element of preparation. Too often though it is immediately identified as weight training. Weights both free and captive are only a small part of the coach's repertoire. Interestingly, in the DDR heavy weight training was undertaken only by those who had to have absolute strength, such as weightlifters and those involved in throwing activities. Those involved in other sports used their own bodyweight, often using simple equipment in a multitude of sport-specific ways to develop the exact type of strength required, as typified by the Jumping and Throwing Decathlons.

Similarly with flexibility training. All sports require mobility to some extent! Each sport will be specific and each will have identified exercises and drills to develop that facility. It is the pre-puberty period that is the cause for concern with this type of work. The musculo-skeletal systems can easily be damaged if habitual ranges of movement are exceeded. All mobility work must be supervised. Post-puberty mobility work must be included in some form or another to develop range of movement and in the prevention of injury.

It is assumed that all training and competitive activity will begin with a sport-specific warm-up. This is not only good practice in preparing the body for the stresses of exercise, it can enhance performance and reduce injuries. Most sports have specific regimes that relate to their very specific needs of which all coaches are fully aware. It is also assumed that all activity will finish with a cool-down to enable the body to recover from the session and to speed recovery and adaptive processes.

SPORT-SPECIFIC SCHEDULE

Rugby Union

Pre-Season

Sunday	Rest
Monday	Strength training
Tuesday	5 km jog
Wednesday	Interval training using fitness centre equipment
Thursday	Strength training
Friday	Repeat Tuesday's or Wednesday's session
Saturday	5 km jog and strength training

Early Season

Sunday	Match
Monday	Rest or 3K jog
Tuesday	3 km jog and strength training
Wednesday	Club – technical and tactical training
Thursday	3 km jog and strength training
Friday	3 km jog and speed training
Saturday	Rest

Mid to End of Season

Sunday Match or technical and tactical training
Monday Speed training
Tuesday 3 km jog and strength training
Wednesday Speed training and light strength training
Thursday Agility and speed work
Friday Technical and tactical training
Saturday Rest

Rowing

Pre-Season

Sunday Rowing sustained 70 per cent effort for 10 km+
Monday 5 km+ jog and strength training
Tuesday Rowing sustained 70 per cent effort for 10 km+
Wednesday 7 km+ jog and strength training
Thursday Rest
Friday 7 km+ jog and strength training
Saturday Rowing sustained 70 per cent effort for 10 km+

Early Season

Sunday Rowing 2 × 1.5 km at 90 per cent
Monday Strength training
Tuesday Rowing 3 × 4 minutes at 90 per cent
Wednesday Rowing intervals – 2 × 10 periods of alternating 30 seconds hard/easy at 90 per cent
Thursday Rowing sustained effort 70 per cent for 10 km+
Friday Rowing 5 × 3 minutes at 90 per cent
Saturday Technical session – clock session 2 × 3, 2, 1 minutes at 85 per cent

Mid to End of Season

Sunday Rowing 2 × 1.5 km at 90 per cent
Monday Strength training
Tuesday Rowing 3 × 10 minutes at 85 per cent
Wednesday Rowing intervals – 2 × 10 periods of alternating 30 sec hard 20 sec easy at 90 per cent

Thursday	Rowing 3 × 5 minutes at 90 per cent
Friday	Rowing technical session – clock session 2 × 3, 2, 1 minutes at 85 per cent
Saturday	Rowing intervals 2 × 12 periods of alternating 20 sec hard 15 sec easy at 90 per cent

Track and Field

1500 m athlete

Pre-Season

Sunday	45 min Fartlek
Monday	7 km sustained run and strength training
Tuesday	6–10 × 400 m at 70 sec
Wednesday	45 min Fartlek and circuit training
Thursday	3–5 × 600 m at 70 sec/400 m pace
Friday	Rest
Saturday	Race or 7 km cross country

Early Season

Sunday	Easy 30 min Fartlek
Monday	3 km sustained. 5 × 300 m at 44 sec and strength training
Tuesday	10 × 400 m at 65 sec
Wednesday	4 × 800 m at 2 min 15 sec and circuits
Thursday	16 × 200 m at 30 sec
Friday	Rest
Saturday	Race or 1200 m time trial, even pace 3 min 15 sec

Mid to End of Season

Sunday	Easy 30 min Fartlek
Monday	3 km sustained. 5 × 300 m at 42 sec and strength training
Tuesday	10 × 400 m at 63 sec
Wednesday	4 × 800 m at 2 min 10 sec
Thursday	30 min Fartlek
Friday	Rest
Saturday	Race

Association Football

Pre-Season

Sunday	Club – basic skills development
Monday	Strength training
Tuesday	5 km jog
Wednesday	3 km sustained effort run and circuit training
Thursday	Club – basic skills development
Friday	5 km jog and strength training
Saturday	Rest

Early Season

Sunday	Match
Monday	Rest or 3 km jog
Tuesday	Club – personal skill development
Wednesday	5 km sustained effort run and strength training
Thursday	Club –technical and tactical training
Friday	3 km jog and speed training
Saturday	Rest

Mid to End of Season

Sunday	Match
Monday	Speed training
Tuesday	3 km jog and strength training
Wednesday	Club
Thursday	Club – technical and tactical training
Friday	3 km jog
Saturday	Rest

CHAPTER 10
ADAPTED TRAINING

The popular notion of elite performers in any sport tends to identify specific stereotypes. The ancient Greek statue of Discobolus has been used down the centuries to portray the ideal physique of any athlete. During the Renaissance Michelangelo's David saw fit to reinforce the classical concept of the Adonis as the iconic symbol of male strength and power. It is interesting to note that very little classical or renaissance art depicts women in a similar manner. The ancient Olympic Games were only for men though eventually the women had a (very limited) opportunity to display their athletic skills in ceremonies in praise of the goddess Hera. However, in most cases it is only in the last one hundred years that women have been given similar opportunities as men in sport and life in general. The concept of 'equal opportunities' is a recent and still evolving one.

It is a fact that the development of women's sport has been hampered by cultural, political and social stereotyping since time out of mind. And, some might say that there is still a long way to go to achieve both the opportunities and recognition accorded to their male counterparts. If approximately 50 per cent of the population have had to, and still do, suffer from discrimination, what of other groups? There has of late been a more enlightened willingness to integrate and engage individuals and groups from a wide range of backgrounds and abilities into society in general and sport in particular.

Equal opportunities provision is being developed throughout the world, principally in countries adopting and implementing the United Nations Charter on Human Rights. In a sporting context it is acknowledged that it is a fundamental right of everyone, irrespective of age, sex, race, culture, religion, means or ability, to have the opportunity to take part in sport and physical activity and to experience and enjoy the benefits of participation. As social and cultural changes evolve elements of the population currently disenfranchised will become enabled and empowered in the sporting context.

However, not everyone has the physique of the classical athlete, male or female! That in itself may influence the opportunities that are made available to people. But what of a largely ignored part of society, those individuals that have some form of impairment or special need? It is estimated that in the UK two out of every five citizens have a recognised impairment, a disability that has an impact on the quality of their daily life. The condition could be associated with mobility, getting up and down stairs, walking, limited sight or poor hearing. It might be in the form of an illness such as diabetes or as a result of a transplant. It might be of a more obvious physical nature such as a missing limb or paraplegia. It is unthinkable in this enlightened age that any such individuals should be discriminated against in their efforts to participate in physical activity.

The Paralympic Vision

The motivation, commitment, dedication and success of this large part of our society has now been recognised by the ultimate sports body, the International Olympic Committee. They have created the Paralympics as a stage for all impaired sportsmen and women to compete at the highest level of international sport, just like the able-bodied, and, in so doing, have recognised that there is no stereotypical image of an Olympic champion, such as Discobolus, that exclusive icon of physical perfection. Olympic success is now available to any sportsman or woman who is willing to endure the years of dedication and sacrifice to rigours of training and preparation. All involved in sport as administrators, officials and coaches together with facility providers must identify that their efforts should be directed to all participants and not exclusive individuals or groups.

Participation in sport or physical activity should be made available for the whole population. Similarly opportunities, resources and coaching should not be available solely to the able-bodied or exclusive groups. 'Sport for All' should be the motto of every governing body. Individuals with disabilities are not automatically thought of as part of a nation's sporting elite; however, they have the same rights and expectations with regard to opportunities and coaching in sport.

Involvement in sport does not merely offer the obvious opportunities for enjoyment and success, but provides a whole raft of associated benefits such as social interaction, a healthier lifestyle, a sense of well-being, adventure, excitement, challenge, fun and enjoyment. Role models such as Tanni Grey-Thompson have brought the sporting success of Paralympians to the notice of the general public. Her success in the Olympic Games, London Marathon and other international meetings has done much to put disability sport on the mainstream agenda. Through the process each individual has the opportunity to experience emotional highs and lows and develop personal qualities of self-confidence, self-worth and self-image, all in a controlled and supportive environment. Carefully planned, activity, training sessions and a competitive environment will serve to enhance the quality of life for *all* athletes. It clearly follows therefore that coaching champions is a concept that includes *all* athletes.

All champions are people! They all have their strengths and weaknesses, good points and bad points. Sport is not a level playing field. Not all athletes are born with equal abilities and qualities; with special groups particular strategies may need to be considered. As the Paralympic movement progresses there is more attention being paid to the development of coach education to provide a better service for athletes with special abilities. However, though you may not have specific qualifications to coach disabled sportsmen and women, sport-specific knowledge and understanding combined with commitment to the coaching process is a solid start.

Any experienced coach will say that she or he coaches athletes – people, not the sport-specific skills! All athletes have strengths and weaknesses. It is the relationship between coaches and athletes that develops a strategy to enable performance to progress. There is no difference when working with athletes with 'recognised' disabilities. From a personal perspective my own involvement with disabled athletes has been rewarding and has improved my coaching performance. Sometimes accepted coaching skills do not work. How do you demonstrate throwing the discus to a blind athlete? How do you give relevant and meaningful feedback?

A Practical Example

My experience with one of my athletes might illustrate the point. Steve was totally blind and had no experience of throwing the discus at all, but he wanted to learn. Initially when we began to work together I had to physically place him in a throwing position. Over a period of time he began to 'feel' where his feet, upper body and arms were. Instead of showing him, together we developed a system whereby after a throw I would make a comment, and if he felt it was needed we would compare his thinking of what he was doing to the actuality. To ensure he was throwing in the right direction Steve came up with idea of putting a towel on the floor in front of his forward foot – simple, but effective. Steve was a competent thrower and entered many competitions for both blind and able-bodied with a degree of success.

All athletes want to improve – they are ambitious. So it was with Steve. He knew from 'talking books' and other athletes that he was performing only part of the complete technique. He wanted to do the full thing, which involves turning and movement across the circle before the final throwing phase. With no sight there are no points of reference! How do you know where to stand? When to start to turn? When have you turned enough to move to the front of the circle? How do you know you are at the front of the circle? How do you know which direction to throw? Steve and I worked together and solved all the issues. I would position him at the back of the circle, then he was on his own. Over a period of time we broke the technique into parts and he mastered each one, then we put the parts together in one (sometimes) flowing movement! That process is exactly the same with every discus thrower. Steve was no different. With his advanced technique his performances improved, as did his success.

There were several unexpected and surprising benefits of working with Steve. First I had to re-evaluate what actually were the *essential* aspects of the technique, not the frilly bits that look impressive but do not contribute to performance. Through this process I began to appreciate the simplicity of what is deemed to be a complicated technique. I had to adopt a clearer and simpler way of explaining, and develop more practical ways of ensuring that athletes could feel the whole throwing process. All my athletes benefited.

Initially I worked on a one-to-one basis with Steve because he thought he would feel uncomfortable with 'more able athletes'. However he soon joined my group of throwers. Though he was quickly welcomed into the group there was a tension because they had no experience of blind people, let alone blind athletes. It took very little time for them to accept Steve as a competent athlete, just like them. Soon they were guiding him out to collect his discoi. He had no special treatment. They took over the coaching role. Without thinking they would help Steve into the circle, give him feedback and develop a hands-on approach. He became involved in club activities and educated everyone on the potential of all athletes. In an athletic and social sense my athletes and everyone at the club, especially me, benefited more from the situation than Steve did! My advice to any coach who has the opportunity to work with 'disabled' athletes is to grasp the opportunity. It is challenging, rewarding, beneficial and enlightening in every way.

Definition of Terms

An understanding of some of the additional factors a coach needs to consider when planning, preparing and delivering a training programme might be useful.

Often descriptors such as disability and handicap are used to mean the same thing, a condition that negatively affects performance. If we are to understand better how the coach can create individual programmes we need a clearer definition of terms.

Impairment includes any psychological, physiological or anatomical dysfunction, abnormality, defect, or limb or organ loss.

Disability includes the loss or reduction of functional ability and activity as a result of impairment.

A Handicap is the disadvantage in performance as a result of impairment and disability.

But, like all things in life, it is not that simple. Any departure from the 'norm' can range from being so slight that it is virtually undetectable to being extremely severe; or it might not affect performance at all.

Physical disability affects any movement and coordination.

Sensory disability affects the senses, usually vision or hearing.

Paraplegia is the loss of use of the legs as a result of spinal cord damage. There may be an associated loss of ability that will be greater the higher the site of the spinal cord injury.

An amputee has lost one limb or more, or part of a limb.

Les autres is a catch-all term used to categorise all disabilities that do not have specific definition, such as poliomyelitis.

Hidden impairments are a wide range of conditions that do not restrict movement but can affect performance, such as epilepsy or transplants.

Apart from medical or physical constraints to movement there is a series of mental conditions that can equally affect performance. There is now a catch-all term used to identify this group, **Learning difficulty**. The term is generally used to refer to an impairment of the intellectual capacity or function of an individual, from whatever cause.

Though most athletes with an impairment will be in a specific category, confusion can arise if they have multiple disabilities such as being diabetic and blind, like Steve.

Each Olympics gives the general population a glimpse of the excellence disabled athletes can achieve. It also serves to identify the potential of all those with a disability who seek to take up sport. With such fantastic role models many youngsters who would never have thought of participating in sport are now doing so and have the same expectations in terms of their performance development as anyone else. Stereotypes have to be dismissed. Not all disabled individuals use wheelchairs! Just because someone is described as disabled does not mean they are stupid!

Coaches and those involved in sport have to broaden their perspective as to the nature of disability and the potential of athletes. Rewards of success, though slow in coming, are now percolating the ranks of disabled sport. Training grants, sponsorship, product association and cash incentives are now available. Paralympics are raising the profile of disabled athletes on a par with their able-bodied counterparts, though total equality is yet to be achieved. The motivation, commitment and determination of disabled athletes is exactly the same as that of the able-bodied. The coaching process of talent identification and performance development is the same for everybody. Theories of periodisation of training including strength, speed, suppleness, stamina and skill development are similarly applicable. All athletes are athletes!

THE COACHING PROCESS

The key to successful coaching is the ability to relate to the athlete. Paramount above all skills is the capacity to communicate at a level that is appropriate to their understanding, maturity and practical competence. With particular individuals or teams the coach might adopt additional or alternative strategies, such as the use of audiotapes with blind athletes, or, where there are facilities, presenting information in Braille. For some athletes specific drills or skills might be recorded on videotape. With modern information technology the internet offers a whole range of readily adaptable formats. Of course, these tools can be used with all athletes to some degree. And that is the reality: particular strategies for particular individuals are geared to enabling them to improve their performance and personal development. Strategies tailored for a blind athlete might be equally effective with an able-bodied individual. Effective coaching creates a process that enables the athlete to maximise potential; there is no strategy specific for the blind, deaf, paraplegic or amputee. It is an enriching process for the coach to develop a battery of innovative – not to say strange – ways of coaching which, designed for one individual, can be extremely helpful to others.

A Practical Example

Some years ago I was involved with a Ju-Jitsu Black Belt grading. The candidates were assembled on the mat and were taken through a series of techniques and one-on-one attack and defence scenarios. All went well. The group were working as a unit, everyone responding to a given instruction in unison, correctly. No one stood out as being better or worse than the rest. In fact they were all a credit to their instructors. The final part of their grading was a *kata*, a complicated sequence of attack and defence techniques against an imaginary attacker. The movements are strictly choreographed and may involve as few as twenty to over a hundred techniques, all of which have to be produced in an exact order. Each candidate performs the *kata* on his own (on this occasion they happened to be all males) in the middle of a square, matted area. All the other candidates, coaches, parents, wives, partners, children, friends, general spectators and the senior instructors assessing the grading watch – a very nerve-racking experience for anyone. Halfway through, the Dojo (training hall) went quiet. An anticipation of something special ran through the spectators.

David, a young man who had walked confidently on to the mat, went through the *kata* flawlessly if slightly more slowly than the rest. The grading continued. All students passed the examination. The final ceremony was the presentation of the coveted black belts to all the successful candidates. Each in turn walked forwards, bowed and received the black belt from the senior instructor. When it was David's turn the Dojo erupted! He was well known to everyone there because of his long association with the club. Everyone enjoyed his success, especially his parents.

After the event I chatted with the senior instructor and, of course, David's performance was mentioned. I commented that though perfect, David's *kata* was marginally slower than the rest. The senior instructor paused, and said that David had learning difficulties, but, seeming a little embarrassed he went on, 'Ah! You noticed! Well, that was my fault. I recorded the names of the techniques in order, with changes in direction, on an audiotape, and gave it to David. When he practised the *kata* he used a Walkman so that he could learn to perform the techniques in order and correctly, according to my instructions. Because I made the mistake of speaking too slowly on the tape, David performed them at my speed. My fault, it won't happen next time. I'll talk faster!'

Coaching athletes with learning difficulties might seem daunting, but it can be yet another learning curve. Coaches have to consider the language they use, and identify the basic concepts of technique and performance. Being constantly conscious of language and terminology makes you realise just what you are saying! What might be perfectly clear to you in your own mind might not be communicated to others. With *any* athlete the coach has to use language appropriate to his or her intellectual and technical understanding. Similarly, complex skills are broken down into a sequence of simple ones, each one easy to learn, and are then assembled into a whole action. Do not use jargon! What I mean by a 'shift' across the circle in shot-put does not equate to normal language. Textbooks and other coaches might use different words, so: KIS (Keep it Simple)! If athletes without learning difficulties find it difficult to know exactly what you mean there is something lacking with the way you communicate. As coaches we sometimes get caught up in our own comfort zone of jargon. It keeps us smug and gives us a feeling of power!

Visual Impairment

All athletes should be protected from possibly hazardous situations, but with particular individuals or groups additional care may need to be taken. As an example, blind athletes have an obvious disadvantage. Often coaches fail to understand that, away from sport, for the rest of their day, week and life, visually impaired athletes manage very well in the world. But, in an artificial situation such as sport there are unique hazards, and, in many cases they are additionally hampered by the lack of their guide dog or cane. This is not a very hospitable environment. Keep the training and competition areas clear of debris – a good tip for those who can see as well!

Sound is an important tool for a blind athlete. A noise can be used to indicate direction. Balls can have a bell or buzzer in them for location. Giving simple commands such as 'left' or 'right' allows athletes to run in a straight line. Do not shout! Speak to all athletes in a tone and volume appropriate to the situation. If needed, draw word pictures, and try to communicate images that the athlete can understand. By mutual consent, agree to a system of physically positioning an athlete or guiding him or her through a movement to enable them to 'feel' it. Take care not to dominate the situation! You will often be asked to put the athlete in the right position, or to be guided from a to b, and will be told how to do it. If in doubt, ask. If athletes have residual vision, make the best of it. Use brightly coloured equipment and stand with your back to the light source. I give a comprehensive training programme to all my athletes. Peter, another blind athlete, persuaded his wife to audiotape the details for him to follow.

Hearing Impairment

Hearing impaired athletes give the coach yet another opportunity to think about what they say and do. Make sure the athletes can see your face clearly – facial expressions carry as much information as does lip reading. To attract their attention, be prepared to touch them in an appropriate manner. Try learning sign language. My attempts usually ended in convulsions of laughter!

Physical Disability

Those athletes with normal hearing and vision, without learning difficulties, but with some physical disability will tend to challenge the coach in a different manner. Often a technique or tactic will have to be modified to very specific individual physical constraints. The coach has to use every faculty the athlete possesses to maximise performance: 'Don't patronise. Utilise!'

One of the biggest obstacles to participation in sport and general social inclusion is access. Many forms of transport, buildings, sports and training facilities are not user-friendly for those with specific needs. Thankfully the Disability Discrimination Act of 2000 has set the wheels rolling to ensure that every member of society has equal ease of access and opportunities.

CHAPTER 11
SAFE COACHING

It can be appreciated that the coaching of champions is subject to a great many influences. There are many individuals and organisations that contribute to the process and the final outcome. Implicit in the process is that the interest of the player is uppermost in everyone's mind, and that any decision-making includes the athlete concerned at all times. Coercion is not an option.

EARLY DAYS

Potential champions may begin their path to success in early childhood when they are under the influence, guidance and protection of the family. Through play in a safe and enjoyable environment a wide range of intellectual, social and physical skills develop. In this situation parents can control the amount of time given to play and what it entails. Play should be enjoyable and fun. It is not work! During the early years not only are embryonic skills developed but, perhaps more importantly, positive attitudes to learning are inculcated.

Over-enthusiasm or too zealous an approach from excessively ambitious parents might create an initial boost to performance that is all too frequently ephemeral. It is more likely to create within the child an antagonism towards the activity for the rest of their lives and create negative attitudes towards those concerned. Though some parents have a background in physical education, most do not. Being an arm-chair sports critic is not the same as having a depth of knowledge, understanding and competence in coaching generally or working with youngsters specifically.

One father I met told me that his 7-year-old was going to be an Olympic 1500 metres champion, and he wanted me to coach him. His son he said, with glowing pride, was a 'good runner'. He went on to extol the virtues of the training of a recent Olympian which he had read about in a magazine. He had studied the training schedules very carefully and had come to the conclusion that because his son was so 'gifted' he would follow the programmes of the champion when he was 17! The boy was too young to compete in organised competitions and he felt that I and the governing body could open doors for him. No amount of persuasion on my part could convince the father that perhaps the youngster was too young for such an appraisal of his ability and certainly not physically mature enough to participate in such a strenuous programme of work.

For the next few weeks the father with his son in tow did the rounds of the local coaches and clubs. The father pestered the regional and national administration and individual national coaches trying to pressurise them into following his way of thinking. Then, they were gone! Nothing was ever heard of the father or the son again. The embryonic Olympian never fulfilled his father's expectations. A possible elite performer was lost to the sport by unrealistic expectations. Fortunately these examples are few and far between. There are examples of parents successfully coaching their children but these instances really are rare. The pressures generated on all concerned tend to produce a mutually disadvantageous situation at best and emotional disaster at worst.

Most parents of talented youngsters in the 7–9 age range tend to become involved with local clubs. Primary schools tend not to have the resources or the expertise to develop specific talents. Following the generic structure of the national curriculum for all abilities and inclinations tends to consume the staff time available and any resources. This general development of a wide range of motor skills at this age, not specialisation, follows the guidelines for best practice set out by most expert opinion. Even so most primary schools can and do identify pupils with exceptional ability and in the main liaise with parents and local clubs.

Once a link has been set up between the local club and coach the role of the parent is very important. Many coaches see caring or ambitious parents as one of the main barriers to overcome! Coaches see themselves as the experts and want to get on with the process of working with young players in their own way. The fact of the matter is that both parties are equally important in the development of a child's sporting talent. The family provide a caring and supportive homelife which will involve a commitment from themselves to take their child to training and competitions, pay for additional travel to events, training, match and tuition fees, provide specialist clothing and equipment and be supportive in times of success and failure. Such a commitment of resources impacts not only on parents but also on other members of the family. Generally the result is cutbacks in family expenditure and outlays of time that will affect holidays and every other member of the family.

The pressure that a youngster feels, or is, in some cases, made to feel, can be enormous: a sense of relief when successful, tremendous guilt in failure.

A friend of mine was an elite middle distance athlete as a youngster. When he won, as he often did, his parents were so proud and glowed when bragging to family and friends about the success of their son and how it was all down to their sacrifice. When he lost a race they would not speak to him for days and sometimes weeks. It was also pointed out to the youngster that he was ungrateful for the deprivations that they were enduring for his selfish pleasures.

With such an investment of personal and family resources, parents want to be involved in the sporting development of their child. The coach and parents must, for the sake of the child, identify a mutually agreeable policy. With most parents they are only too pleased to allow the 'professional' to guide them. Parents should be given a regular update on training and competition and opportunities to discuss issues. Too often this lack of communication can be seen at fixtures with eager parents shouting inappropriate comments at their child or taking side-swipes at their state of preparation. Many coaches provide detailed documentation of training session, fees, personal equipment, fixtures and other related material. Families have to plan to take children to games and training! They also have to ensure that family life, school and support are kept in balance. Ideally with such a coordinated approach everyone should be happy.

Parental Expectations of Coaches

- to look after their children as if they were their own, *in loco parentis*
- to include parents in the whole training and competitive process
- to adopt a child-centred programme that identifies the needs and aspirations of the child first and last
- to include the child in the process of planning and preparation
- to conduct themselves in a thoroughly professional manner at all times
- to develop training strategies that are appropriate to the ability and inclination of the child
- to give an occasional reality check.

Coaches' Expectations of Parents

- to treat them as professionals
- to support their decisions and actions
- not to have unrealistic expectations of their child
- not to have unrealistic expectations of the coach
- to provide a stable base in which they and their child can maintain a sense of proportion and enjoy success and cope with defeat
- to provide information on any problems at home or school which might impact on performance
- to give them an occasional reality check.

THE COACH

The significance of parents in the nurturing of young sportsmen and women is self-evident – it is critical! The foundations for further development of individual skills and any ultimate achievements are established in the early years of childhood. However, sooner or later it will become necessary to seek the help of an expert within the sport. This individual is usually ascribed the title of coach but there are others that are used such as teacher, trainer or instructor.

Titles aside, the background, training and experience of coaches is obviously a very important issue. What makes someone want to coach? The fact is that there seem to be tens of thousands of individuals who want to pass on their skills and knowledge to others. As to whether they are all equally competent with all ages, abilities and ambitions is far from clear. It is also clear that it is vital to find a coach with the skills to enable developing talent. There is a debate among academics as to the nature of coaching whether it is a precise science or an art (figure 11.1). The reality is that it is both. So who are these gifted individuals who coach?

Former Players

Coaches who fall into this category have personal knowledge, understanding and underpinning practical skills; however, their own experiences within the sport will greatly influence their attitude and philosophy. Those who themselves were former champions may have difficulty in working with lesser mortals. Elite performers tend to be those who possess a single-minded determination, commitment and tenacity to succeed, and they are gifted with natural ability. For these

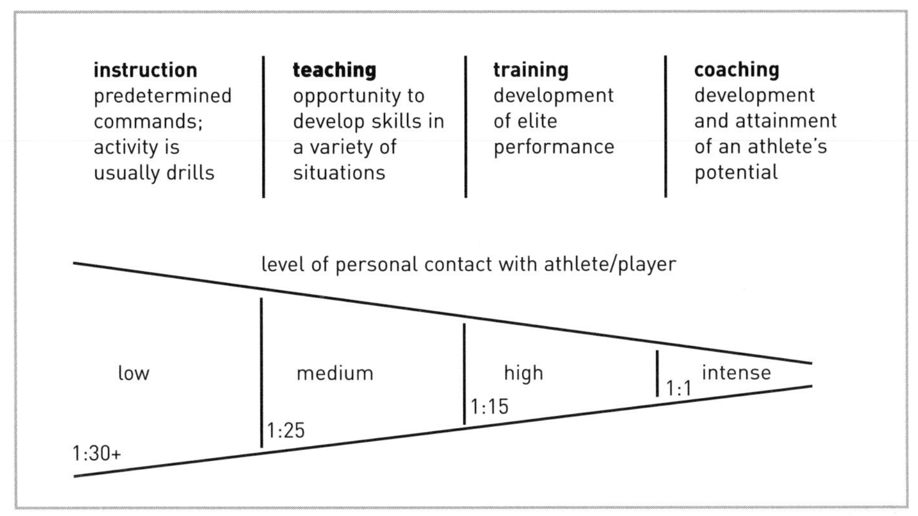

FIG. 11.1 Often the titles used in sport relate to the numbers involved.

individuals the learning of skills is easy, and often difficulties arise when they work with slower learners or under-achievers. Coaches who were keen if less talented players tend to be able to identify with the often arduous process of improving performance. Having experienced setbacks and personal difficulties they may have an insight into the mind of the athlete when dealing with the lows of training and competition. Obviously they are also limited by their own experiences and may not fully appreciate the demands made on and by elite athletes. Whatever the sporting background of a coach, it is no indication of their ability to pass on their knowledge and experience to others in an effective, efficient and safe manner.

The ideal coach is the one who can enable a player to achieve his or her potential. Former participants tend to focus on the particular aspects that they enjoyed or in which they were particularly successful. They may not be able or even wish to offer a comprehensive programme of help and advice, seeking only to operate in specific aspects of performance. For example, not all athletics coaches teach every event; they tend to specialise in specific groups, e.g. jumps, hurdles or throws, while others may focus on a single activity such as the hammer throw. In football one coach may specialise in developing goalkeeping skills, while another develops specific attacking or defending techniques and tactics. In American football training there are coaches assigned to every position; some have expertise in attacking play while others specialise in defence. The development of positional coaches within the game situation is becoming more prevalent. Obviously the potential champion needs to be working as early as possible with the coach who has the ability to meet very specific requirements. The qualities of being a former player do not automatically equip someone to coach. Most governing bodies now realise that a formal coaching qualification provides the coach with the communication skills to put the message across effectively.

Teachers of Physical Education

Following the early experiences of skill development within the family setting the usual scene of progress for most youngsters is within the school curriculum. Most countries have some form of national curriculum for physical education and they tend to follow a similar pattern. Youngsters are exposed to a wide variety of physical activity designed to establish a comprehensive repertoire of general skills, including performing single and linked skills and to develop endurance, strength, mobility, agility and games skills, all of which are refined in a systematic and progressive way throughout school life. Physical activity is also seen as a way of developing personal qualities such as the ability to work with others, an appreciation of the aesthetic qualities of movement, the development of decision-making skills and the experience of leadership.

The development of an individual's specific talent is not on the main agenda, especially in the early years. In fact it is often frowned upon as being at odds with the development of their more academic profile. Later, especially with some of the schools who have achieved specialist status, pupils may be offered limited opportunity for their own personal development. The reality is that the training of physical educationalists is focused on the pedagogical process and child development. Though there is an element of practical work in their studies it is of a general nature to enable the development of basic skills to facilitate the teaching of a wide range of sports.

Within this process there is no specialisation, therefore the physical educationalist may not have the specific sporting knowledge to enable particular individuals. Trainee and qualified PE teachers have to attend national governing body coaching courses to pick up sport-specific expertise. When in post, most specialist teachers of physical education create links with a wide range of sports clubs, who often make use of the school's facilities, and are well placed to introduce talented individuals to clubs and coaches. The schools very often provide the progressive link between home, school, club and coach on the talent identification and performance development ladder.

With the opportunities for personal and financial success developing at a rate of knots it is becoming increasingly more apparent that all of those involved in the development of sporting talent should be well-educated and well-trained. In recent years efforts have been made to use the skills of doctors, surgeons, pharmacologists, physiologists, psychologists and psychiatrists, sociologists, nutritionalists, physicists, biomechanics specialists, engineers and educationalists in an attempt to improve performance. From this great wealth of science- and sport-related knowledge has emerged a vast amount of information to enable the maximisation of performance.

It has also become evident that the days of the well-meaning adviser with little technical or sport-related expertise are rapidly running out. It has become apparent that all who wish to help in the development of sporting talent should themselves go through a process of training. Because of the very specific demands of individual activities the various national governing bodies of sport have the responsibility for training their coaches. Several years ago I devised a four-level coach education programme which seems to embrace most of the requirements identified.

Level 1 Assistant Coach – an elementary course covering elementary coaching skills.

This is the first rung on the coaching ladder and enables aspiring individuals to work under the direction of the session coach, assisting in the delivery of planned activity. This first level involves 'workplace experience' under the guidance of a senior coach, where they will develop the competence to:

- work closely with and under the guidance of the session coach
- demonstrate and explain basic techniques and tactics
- identify errors and suggest methods of correction
- give appropriate feedback to participants
- reinforce good performance with praise
- develop coaching styles to suit different situations
- develop an effective working relationship with the participants and others involved in the process

- ensure maximum participation and enjoyment
- prepare participants for training – warm-up
- cool down participants after training.

Related Health and Safety legislation will be included in best practice in all of these elements and governing body specific requirements. Experience gained at this level acts as a foundation for further progression if so desired.

Level 2 Intermediate Coach – an 'improvers' course that builds on personal competencies and develops technical knowledge.

Having gained experience and confidence at level 1 the coach may seek to progress to planning, preparing and delivering a session him- or herself, without supervision. Obviously to work unsupervised an additional repertoire of capabilities is needed which includes understanding of:

- the national structure of the sport, including competition structure, talent identification, performance development, selection strategies and coaching support
- the overall nature of the coach's job
- how the coach behaves – a code of ethics
- the responsibilities of the coach
- how to coach
- the screening of new players
- the need for warm-up and cool-down – a basic understanding of related sports science
- training safety
- how to deal with emergencies
- sport and the law – an overview of issues including child protection, disability discrimination, social inclusion and equal opportunities.

During the training period surrounding the attainment of this level the coach will also improve the range and depth of her or his knowledge of sport-specific techniques and tactics, which will enable them to work with better performers.

Level 3 Competent Coach – for the individual who seeks to organise the training of individuals or teams and may be responsible for running a club, or teams and organising other coaches. Sport-specific knowledge and skills obviously need to be developed to meet the players' demands as well as administrative and management ability to ensure the success of their team or club. Topics will include:

- effective coaching – techniques and tactics
- how to monitor and measure fitness
- how to set targets and plan training
- how to improve performance – planning training
- reviewing the programme
- how to coach children and young performers
- working with specific groups – social inclusion
- counselling athletes
- opening, promoting and developing a club
- managing the club
- organising courses and events.

Level 4 Advanced Coaching Award – at this level coaches may be seeking to specialise in particular aspects such as working with young players, talent identification, elite performers and national squads. With the wide range of sports science inputs they might wish to develop particular areas such as strength training, nutrition or technical analysis. This specialisation may simply be for personal satisfaction or as part of the governing bodies' performance development policy. The delivery of these elements may be part of the sport's education programme or involve linking in with colleges, universities and other agencies who have the expertise. Topics may include:

- the philosophy of coaching
- the identification and development of sporting excellence
- the development of mobility
- the development of strength
- the development of speed

- the development of endurance
- the periodisation of training
- the biomechanical analysis of performance
- nutrition
- factors affecting performance.

Governing bodies usually encourage coaches to produce a coaching log of their planning, preparation and delivery of individual sessions as part of an overall training programme. Coaches are monitored and mentored throughout the whole process by suitably qualified personnel who guide them through their personal development. Governing bodies award coaches qualifications that will enable them to operate at the level to which they aspire within the sport. With the governing body coaching award and log as evidence of their practical competence, coaches can seek to have their qualifications recognised as formal vocational qualifications.

In many sports the process of talent identification, performance development and coach education are well established. Despite the various agendas of parents, coaches, governing bodies and the athlete themselves it has long been held that the interests, welfare and well-being of the individual are paramount. Unfortunately, as in all walks of life there are those who would seek to manipulate a situation for their own benefit no matter what the cost to others, and sport is no exception. Thankfully, these situations are few and far between, but when they do arise they can have a devastating impact on the athlete and long-term consequences for everyone concerned and the sport itself. However, in the eagerness to achieve excellence youngsters can unwittingly be vulnerable and easy prey to those who would wish to exploit them.

The national figures for *recorded* instances of child abuse are alarming; one can only guess as to what goes undetected. In 2001 in the UK some 34,000 youngsters were identified as needing protection from abuse. The forms of abuse that children might suffer can fall within a wide range, including racial, cultural, religious, social, financial, emotional and sexual, or treatment inapproriate for their age or physical ability. It is sad but true that in the majority of cases the abuser is well known to the child and often in a position of trust. The incidence of abuse in sport is still an unknown quantity, but the fact that cases are reported in the media from time to time indicates that there is a potential problem. As with society in general, all those involved with the care of youngsters should seek to offer a safe and protective environment for their development.

Those who work in sport are in a privileged position. Parents put their trust in coaches to develop the athletic potential of their children. It is a great honour and a mark of the level of respect in which they are held. It is self-evident that the coach will seek to ensure that any physical activity is a safe, enjoyable, challenging and rewarding experience for every youngster. The sporting environment away from parents, teachers and other adults is at times quite informal, since part of the learning process is for the personal development of the individual and for them to take responsibility, at least in part, for their actions. Conversations take place between the athlete and coach, players and others involved. In this relaxed atmosphere sport can provide an opportunity to identify those who are being or are at risk of being abused.

Professionals who are charged with the care of children have long been aware of the need for a responsible attitude towards duties. Teachers, and others, operate *in loco parentis*, as caring parents would act towards their child. In the past coaches who work with children have adopted a similar approach to their work. However with high-profile cases achieving national notoriety, what has been accepted as good practice in the past can no longer be left to chance. Legislation has been passed that clearly sets out the responsibilities of those who have contact with children. In sport this includes parents, coaches, officials, administrators, and the governing body, in the context of training, competition and the techniques and tactics appropriate to the children's ability.

There seems to be a general consensus as to the main focus of attention:

- the development of a code of best practice in coaching children
- implementation of structures and systems within sport that will protect children
- awareness of the different forms of abuse
- vigilance to the evidence of abuse
- the taking of appropriate action
- the interdisciplinary dimension – the role of other organisations.

It has been identified that abuse falls into the following general categories:

Neglect. This occurs when adults, possibly parents, do not provide basic physical and emotional requirements. This may cause deterioration in the health of the child and inhibit normal growth. Negligence may involve inadequate nutrition, inadequate accommodation, poor clothing, and general lack of care and protection from harm.

In a sporting context children should be able to train and compete in safety without being exposed to the risk of injury.

Emotional abuse. If children are subjected to an environment that does not provide love, attention or cherishing it is likely to have a deleterious effect on their psychological development. This may manifest itself in the form of direct or indirect suggestions that the child is unloved, inadequate, worthless or failing to meet expectations. Fear in the form of threats or actual physical assault, being shouted at, ridiculed, belittled or humiliated will affect behaviour, making the child anxious and uncomfortable in company.

In a sporting context children should not be exposed to constant criticism, ridicule, emotional blackmail or sanctions and guilt due to lack of success in achieving unrealistic expectations.

Physical abuse. As the term suggests, children are subject to being hit, shaken, smacked, squeezed, bitten, burnt or scalded.

In a sporting context children should not be coerced into training regimes that are inappropriate to their ability or physical maturity. The use of illegal or inappropriate performance-enhancing products is abuse. Children should not be subjected to any form of corporal punishment in the training or competitive environment.

Sexual abuse. Adults might use children to gratify their sexual needs through sexual intercourse and other perversions. This might involve inappropriate touching, using sexually explicit language and showing pornographic images.

In the sporting context the power of an authority figure and the desire of a youngster to please family and coach may create an environment where sexual abuse occurs. Other forms of abuse such as threats or emotional manipulation might be used to develop the activity and keep it a secret.

Bullying. All those who are involved in the coaching process must be aware of the events and behaviour that can cause abuse, and develop organisational and sports-based strategies to guard children. However, as all parents and teachers will testify, often youngsters have to be protected from each other. Within the training or competitive environment bullying can occur. This can take the form of physical, mental or verbal abuse. This can include the child being:

- shunned by some or all of the group
- taunted, teased or called names
- the constant victim of unpleasant practical jokes
- ridiculed and made to feel different and unwelcome
- the focus of malicious slander and lies
- deprived of personal items by theft or damage
- threatened with physical assault
- the victim of actual physical abuse.

Why such behaviour should occur is difficult to identify but is possibly out of jealousy, fear of losing superior 'star' status or special attention or fear of being dropped from the squad. Everyone involved with children must be alert to any behaviour on the part of the victim or the bully and be willing to listen to witnesses of such behaviour. However, it is possible for bullying to be perpetrated by adults on children in exactly the same way. Unfortunately it is human nature that in any organisation adults can be victims of bullying by other adults. Any incident of bullying by anyone focused towards anyone else is abusive. All have a duty of care to protect the victim and deal with the bully in an appropriate manner.

Abuse of vulnerable individuals. One could argue that all young sportsmen and women by virtue of the lack of maturity fall into this category. Though to a greater or lesser degree this might be true there are those who can find themselves at greater risk. Though this might readily be seen to apply to young athletes with learning difficulties it is by no means exclusive to this group. It can occur where youngsters:

- have poor social skills and restricted experience of life in general. This can make it difficult for them to evaluate the behaviour of others towards them. They might be unable to identify what is an abusive situation
- have been conditioned to follow the directives of adults without question
- are not aware that a situation or the behaviour of others is inappropriate
- have a very poor sense of self-worth
- do not have the confidence or are afraid of the repercussions of talking to others about their concerns
- have no one that they feel they can talk to
- may not have the language or communication skills to articulate their concerns
- feel a sense of embarrassment, shame or guilt
- endure the abuse because they are dependent on others, including the abuser, and are practically unable to avoid inappropriate situations
- are conditioned to intrusive physical and social intervention strategies as part of the management of their physical or mental condition
- think that no one will believe them.

In a sporting context abuse could occur if the needs of the individual are subordinate to the demands of the coach or the existing training and competition requirement of a governing body.

Financial abuse. Obviously there are going to be those individuals with limited life skills and self-confidence who are going to be victims of financial abuse. This may be where youngsters are not allowed to spend as they wish, or, by whatever means and for whatever purpose, take or use money for their own ends.

There is, of course, a new form of abuse that may become more prevalent. It is a fact that in the search for talent, clubs, sports scouts, agents and a range of others are identifying potential at an ever earlier age. Financial arrangements are being made on behalf of children by parents, guardians and others. The legality and the morality of such a situation is dubious at best. Obviously such moneys involved should be invested for the child. It can clearly be seen that any such arrangement has elements of abuse in some form or other, irrespective of whether or not it is appropriate or in the best interest of the youngster at the time or in the future.

All sports are now aware of the potential for abusive behaviour of any sort. Coach education programmes now include strategies to ensure that all activities are carried out in a professional and non-abusive manner. Clubs have strategies such as a drop-in box where general and specific comments can be deposited anonymously. Some have a designated coach with responsibility for the welfare of all participants. Governing bodies have helplines for coaches, parents and anyone else to ring for help if they suspect abuse is taking place. There are phone lines set up by sports to enable all athletes, especially children, to speak to someone who cares about their welfare and who will believe what they say and act upon it. There are local authority and national 'child lines' and organisations such as the Samaritans that exist for the sole purpose of protecting vulnerable individuals. Details of contact numbers and specific personnel should be made available to all athletes. They should be convinced that any concerns will be listened to and treated in absolute confidence. It is vital that this process convinces them further that they will have protection from anyone involved and will receive help in overcoming their abuse.

HEALTH AND SAFETY

There are more fundamental aspects that should be self-evident to coaches and parents alike and form part of an essential checklist. Their importance is obvious:

- Screening new students – before joining a club or working with a coach there needs to be an evaluation of the player's general health. Any medical conditions, injuries or disability that might affect safe participation must be made known. If there is any question as to the safe participation of a player a medical certificate must be produced that specifies that it is safe for the player to participate in the designated activity.

- Within the screening process the sporting aspirations of the player need to be assessed.
- Players need to have full details of training sessions and fixtures to enable parents to organise themselves and make other family arrangements.
- During the first session an assessment of the player's competence needs to be made. From this the coach can prepare a systematic and progressive programme of work that will meet the exact needs of the individual. At this stage it is essential that parents are privy to the assessment by the coach so that discussions can take place as to the ability of the player and the commitment needed by all concerned to realise his or her potential.
- The access to any facility must be free of any hazard, especially in winter.
- Prior to any session the coach must check the facility such as pitch, court, track or gymnasium and *any* associated equipment to ensure that it meets Health and Safety requirements and the minimum standards as set out by the governing body. This includes the playing surface, lights and heating where appropriate. Players must not be exposed to potentially hazardous climatic conditions such as heat, cold, rain or gales. All facilities must be adequately ventilated and heated, both for reasons of hygiene and comfort.
- Often when working in sports centres it is assumed that all is well. But the coach *must* check on emergency egress such as fire doors and any specific evacuation procedures and that there are *no* barriers or equipment blocking rapid exit.
- Any items of sport-specific equipment, such as balls, bats, javelins, which are provided by the club or coach or the players themselves *must* be checked prior to use and be appropriate to the specific ability of the player.
- At the start of the session, as part of the general welcome, a register of all those present, players and non-participants, *must* be taken. In the case of an emergency evacuation it will prove invaluable in ensuring all are safe. It will also provide a record of attendance. Parents may drop off their children at a club but the children may

not actually enter the premises and take part. In an emergency it can resolve a series of issues if parents are trying to collect their children. Often, conflict can arise over team selection, the evidence of regular training and playing can be useful in resolving the situation. Similarly the progress of a player can be queried by parents and others, and a detailed attendance/competition record can readily provide the coach with the necessary evidence.

- The coach must know if there are any recent injuries obtained through training or competition or any other activity that may affect a child's participation. This will enable the coach to monitor the situation throughout the session and ensure that the player does not aggravate the condition in any way.
- The coach must ensure that any medication the player needs, such as a nebuliser, has been brought by the player and is readily available on a shelf and clearly marked with the owner's name.
- It is vital that all items of jewellery, including any body piercings, are removed prior to the session and kept in a secure place. The possible injury of the player and others has to be a consideration. What sportsmen and women as seen on television do does not apply in the real world!
- Clothing must be appropriate for the activity. The minimum guidelines for the activity as laid down by the governing body *must* apply.
- Once satisfied with the suitability of all to participate the session *must* begin with a warm-up.
- During the training session *only* those activities, techniques and tactics approved by the governing body can be practised.
- At the end of the session there must be a cool-down period.
- Players should be supervised as they change to go.
- It is essential that all young players are accompanied by a parent or nominated adult when they leave.
- The coach should check for the usual items of clothing and equipment left behind.

- The safety considerations that apply to participants also apply to spectators. It is essential that the training/competition area is not overcrowded and that players or spectators are not in any danger. The Fire Safety and Safety of Places of Sport Act 1987 has two parts, indoors and outdoors, which set out clear requirements. Coaches and event organisers should ensure that they are acquainted with the appropriate legislation.

  Spectators can themselves pose a potential hazard for participants. Abusive remarks can be both offensive and demoralising to players. Intimidation in the form of a barrage of derogatory comments or threats can markedly influence the performance of an athlete or team. It is not uncommon for spectators to remonstrate with referees, players, coaches and other officials. Overzealous encouragement, often demanding unrealistic effort, can equally influence the player and team. Coaches and officials must create a positive and encouraging environment.
- A first-aid kit should be available for the treatment of minor injuries. The contents of the kit should be regularly checked and only used by those who are qualified. It is not appropriate for a coach to give medical advice or perform intervention strategies for which they are not qualified. Clubs and sports centres must have a procedure for dealing with injuries and accidents. There can be designated first aiders and a system to call for emergency services. Any injury or related incidents must be recorded in the club, centre or coach's accident record book.

If the emphasis is placed on safety in this structured way the caring coach and parent should have no difficulty with potential legal implications arising from accidents. Some coaches may see these requirements as too demanding, but for the safety of young participants who do not have the experience or knowledge to recognise a dangerous situation no precaution can be too much effort.

CHAPTER 12
THE TRAINING AND COMPETITION ENVIRONMENT

After all the planning has been made and schedules designed, taking into account every conceivable variable, the athlete and coach have to put it into practice. For this to happen in an effective manner, to optimise all the resources and expertise available to the individual, sessions have to be presented in a pedagogically correct manner. For the coach the planning and writing-up of a session plan clarifies the rationale behind its aims. The constructive process of setting down the sequential progression of work and the manner in which it is organised can identify potential difficulties or weaknesses which less definitive preparation or coaching 'off the cuff' delivery would not detect. The content, form and style of delivery may not be a measure of coaching ability but they indicate the extent to which sessions have been conscientiously prepared. A written record serves as a very useful monitoring tool as to the athlete's response to the work planned. It also provides a reference for reviewing the effectiveness of the training schedule and facilitating any review. It can also be very valuable evidence should any difficulties arise with personnel and agencies involved.

PLANNING THE SESSION

The first considerations in the construction of any session are:

- What is the purpose of the session?
- What previous work am I assuming?
- What is going to happen in the next sessions?

If the coach of an elite athlete cannot answer any of these questions, planning is inadequate and the effectiveness of the whole process is at best less than might be expected.

Training sessions are not a haphazard series of events. They should be a structured experience, which occurs by design not chance, to create the optimum learning and adaptive experience for the individual athlete. Figure 12.1 shows one of the common problems facing a team coach. The team coach has the added responsibility of ensuring that the same is true for every player involved. The art of effective long-term planning and the individual session is to consider it from the learner's point of view.

Session Structure

Training sessions tend to be divided into three broad areas:

1 Introduction – presentation of aim of session and introductory activities.
2 Development – the main work phase.
3 Conclusion – sessions must conclude in a structured manner both physically and psychologically.

The lesson plan

Figure 12.2 illustrates a typical session plan. Different sports have variations on a theme and individual coaches have their own format but all contain the essential details.

Date. Each session should fit chronologically into the overall plan.

Time. The amount of time for a session will influence what can be achieved. An hour may be more than sufficient for younger participants, while an hour and a half or longer may be required for the more advanced.

Number in the group. The number of players dictates the organisation of practice in managing resources to optimise the value of the training experience for each individual. With larger groups the organisation has to allow for the coach to have an input with each participant. A big group will require a more formal and structured arrangement, while smaller numbers allow for a more informal set-up that will also allow greater coach–athlete contact.

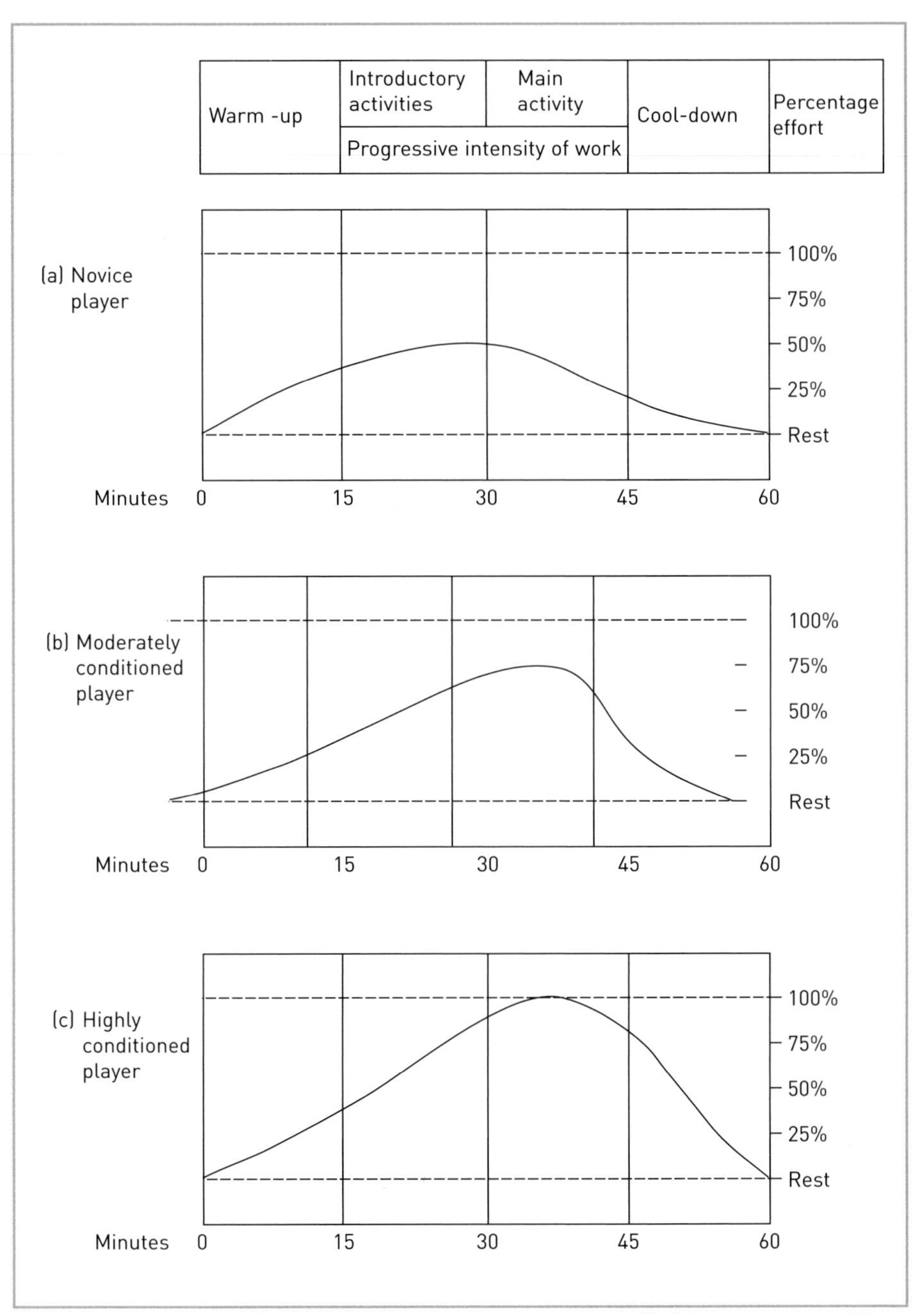

FIG. 12.1 With a mixed ability group the coach has to ensure that all of the group are working at a rate that is suitable for them.

Date	Time	Venue	Number in class
	Duration		Age range
Aim of lesson			Males Females
Special points to note			

	Organisation	Teaching safety points
Introductory activities		
Development		
Conclusion		
Comments		

FIG. 12.2 A typical session plan

Age. It is useful to remember the age range that is being coached. As an aide-mémoire it is a constant reality check on the appropriateness of the training.

Gender. Coaches work with athletes, not males or females. Skill learning is not gender-related, but a coach may wish to consider specific training practices with respect to other relevant issues.

Aim. Every session must have a purpose. You may wish to introduce new ideas or exercises, or revise or continue existing work. The aim of each session has to be carefully identified so that any work covered fits in the correct sequence.

Equipment. Another aide-mémoire to ensure specific pieces of equipment or kit are organised, provided or brought to the session.

Special points. Yet another aide-mémoire! You might need to give out competition or game details or general notices, or to be aware of details of new players, recent results, players who have been injured or ill, aspects of technique or special problems or considerations.

Introductory activities. These might include Health and Safety issues; discussion of previous session; recent results; aims of this session; and any other announcements. Initial contact often sets the tone for the rest of the time. The next element is usually a sport-specific warm-up which is also related to the type of work that will follow. It is essential that the exercises or activities selected for this phase are progressive in terms of technical and physical demands. Often coaches take the opportunity to revise previous sessions' work to a greater or lesser degree as a base for development in this training unit.

Development. Having thoroughly warmed up and worked through technical, tactical or progressive exercises you now have a sound platform from which to initiate the more demanding activity. With new developments it is good practice to refer to previous work of a similar nature and possibly practise that before moving on to the new. It facilitates the effectiveness of learning and general progression moving from the known to the new and increases confidence in a successful progression.

Conclusion. Every session has to have a structured ending and not just be allowed to run out of time. It might run on from the development into a conditioned or full match practice or become a separate element. This might include a fun game activity or more serious fitness and conditioning. But remember that it is essential that sufficient time is left for an adequate cool-down.

Comments. This section allows for an evaluation of how the session went. Critically evaluating the good and not so good aspects will allow for any related modifications in future sessions or general planning. The evaluation might include:

- what was missed out
- which parts were successful or went well
- which parts were unsuccessful or did not go well
- organisation and preparation
- whether the players were challenged
- whether the session achieved its aims
- what the players got out of it
- how the players performed.

By this process of self-evaluation and objectivity you can identify which coaching styles, activities, progressions and lesson contents work and, perhaps more importantly, do not. By reviewing, evaluating and modifying these elements you will refine your coaching ability and technical and tactical competence. The success of any subsequent long-term planning will depend on your ability to assess sessions honestly and critically.

Most committed athletes keep a detailed diary of their training. It is an interesting exercise to compare the work prepared by the coach and how it is evaluated by the performer. In my experience comparing the two records can indicate whether the workload was correct and the desired aims were achieved. Most certainly if training or competitions do not bring about the desired outcomes such a comparison might shed some light on the root causes.

It has always been my practice to give a copy of a training schedule to my athletes. It serves several purposes. It reassures them that work has been prepared to meet their particular requirements and makes them feel important and involved. They also have details of when and where training will be and what it will entail. This is useful in arranging transport and bringing the appropriate kit. Often discussion between athlete and coach can be invaluable in how they perceive a particular block of work.

The early stages of a coach and athlete relationship are characterised by very regular contact; probably every session is supervised but as the athlete matures there may be some that are not. The coach and parents will have to discuss how such sessions will happen. Is there a need for supervision, and if so who will do it or how will it be organised? For example, the athlete may be required to run 5 kilometres and chooses to do it from home or at school. Similarly a strength session might take place at the local sports centre. It is very useful if, in the course of their training diary, the athlete records training details. The athlete can give feedback to the coach by phone, e-mail, or letter, or at the next meeting they can discuss any related issues.

A week-to-view style of diary is usually sufficient but for the more enthusiastic a page a day might be required! Whatever format is chosen the following information, at least, is required.

- Date – this will identify whether or not a session took place. If the athlete does not train as required he or she has to be responsible for his or her actions.
- Time of day and duration of session – was all the work covered? Training immediately after work or school might be the only time available but may not be conducive to the best results.
- Venue – facilities and equipment and therefore being able to complete all tasks may be affected.
- Coach – some clubs might use several coaches. It may well be that a player performs better with a particular coach. Some athletes have more than one coach: technique, tactical or conditioning.
- Introductory activities.
- Development.
- Conclusion.
- Points to remember – what was difficult, what went well and what did not.
- General comments.

The idea of preparing sessions in advance and keeping detailed records might seem an unnecessary burden. However it would be regarded as unacceptable if a schoolteacher when asked replied, 'I am not sure how your child is doing in maths. I don't keep records,' or, 'I do not know when the exams are and have not prepared your child for them.' Sport is no different, particularly when the rewards for success can be as high as through accepted academic routes. The coach has to accept the responsibility which goes with a professional status. Documentation can be invaluable in the monitoring and review process of a programme of work, and can also be a source of reference in resolving issues relating to progress. In the requirements for governing body coaching awards they can serve as evidence of the coach's work leading to her or his formal accreditation.

The Learning Environment

'You can take a horse to water but you cannot make it drink.' The drive of a youngster to improve and willingly work hard to do so is essential. They must possess an intrinsic desire to learn and train, which, nurtured by parents, family and friends, creates the prerequisite foundation for progression and ultimately elite performance. Unfortunately the enthusiasms and desires of parents or family, no matter how well meaning, are no substitute for a lack of personal commitment.

We all improve faster when work has an element of enjoyment and success, and sport is no different. Within the planning of any training or work schedule the coach has to build in opportunities for fun and achievement (figure 12.3). This can be achieved in several ways, including:

- lots of praise for effort or good work
- lots of encouragement
- recognition of effort and improvement
- achievable workloads
- realistic competition targets
- in a team environment, members enabled to support each other.

Motivation. Classically motivation was viewed as having two components:

- internal or intrinsic – the individual's drive to succeed
- external or extrinsic– the influence of others and external factors, such as music, to encourage the player to succeed.

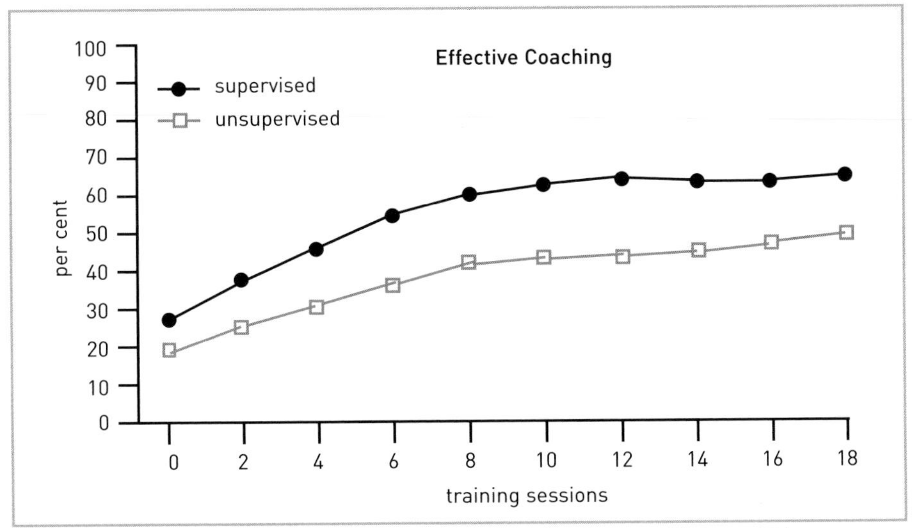

FIG. 12.3 Supervised training sessions are more productive than not. Players will improve without the presence of a coach but not at the same rate. Neither will they achieve their full potential.

As with all things recent studies have suggested other aspects including:

- the drive to achieve success
- the drive to avoid failure.

Youngsters must have the support and encouragement they need to achieve *their* goals. Any training programme must reflect achievable short-, medium- and long-term goals. Whereas youngsters gain a great deal of status from peer group, family and others, great care must be taken to ensure that the aspirations of others are not forced on young performers. Encouragement is not the same as manipulation for one's own ends. Lack of success is not failure, it as an acceptable part of the learning process. It should be viewed as an intrinsic part of sport and as a useful part of the review process.

Youngsters can find themselves in a position of trying to avoid losing so as not to let down and fail family and friends. This is often associated with blaming others ('It wasn't my fault,' 'They wouldn't pass the ball,' 'It was the pitch' or 'It was the ball') or guilt. Any situation that allows this to happen is abusive. The coach, family and friends must have the interest of any player as their sole aim and ensure that such a situation does not occur.

Stress. Selye identified the effect that physical and mental stress has on the individual's response to a given situation. Physical stressors form the underpinning processes of training theory. Similarly with mental stress which is defined as: 'The ability of an individual to respond to the situation which is causing the stress.'

If all preparation has been progressive, and realistic short-, medium- and long-term goals have been achieved, each individual should feel confident in that they are well prepared to deal with a training or competitive situation. If they are not, the coach must look to the planning. No youngster should be exposed to a situation for which they have not been prepared. Such an event might curtail their enthusiasm for the sport and inhibit future involvement.

Arousal or 'psyching' occurs as a response to a given series of stressors. Quite simply it should be sufficient to meet the situation. Too little or too much will markedly affect performance. The training and the preparation process must prepare an individual to meet the exact demands. Conditioned games, time trials, intensive work will ensure that this can occur.

Anxiety or 'competition nerves' are a natural precursor to a challenging situation. The athlete, having been well prepared through progressive work and controlled stressful training, should look on competition as an opportunity to enjoy and succeed. Overanxiety will lead to an overall fall in performance.

There are a series of strategies for dealing with the psychological pressures which can affect performance, such as:

- visualisation
- concentration
- relaxation
- mental rehearsal
- team building
- goal setting
- focusing.

What they do individually or together is to develop a self-confidence in dealing with the challenges athletes or players face. They can be extremely useful tools and I would counsel all coaches and those involved in the coaching process to research their value and application with young athletes. However in most cases they serve to resolve difficulties that arise out of the training programme. If the coach has identified realistic, achievable goals the athlete should be confident that they have been prepared to meet and overcome any situations that their sport presents them.

In other chapters I have described at length the mechanisms for the development of the 'S' factors. However, there is a vital aspect of this process that is rarely considered: the acquisition and refinement of skill. Learning or improving skilful movements is an outward manifestation of a great many anatomical, physiological and neurological processes. Often usually on edited TV highlights, we see examples of great control and coordination. But then the very same player, throughout the rest of the game, given a similar situation, makes a complete hash of things. That movement occurred by chance, not design! Similarly a player, when casually observed, might appear clumsy or uncoordinated but for the rest of the game, when your critical eye is looking elsewhere, shows excellent technique. Skilful movement is that which is the rule not the exception.

The learning and refinement of skills is a long-term process. It depends on the same physiological adaptive processes that improve fitness. It works in the same time-frame. In America, baseball coaches have suggested that it takes one and a half million throws to develop a technically excellent 'pitching' action and related delivery variations. Half a dozen attempts at throwing the javelin or taking penalty kicks is not going to guarantee technical competence or performance.

Technical Development

There are clear progressive stages in the learning and refinement of any movement (figure 12.4):

stage 1	a basic pattern of movement
stage 2	a crude attempt at the technique
stage 3	technical refinement
stage 4	adaptation
stage 5	physiological adaptation

FIG. 12.4 The stages of technical development

1 **Have a go!** Trial and error. Much effort, little recognisable activity.
2 **A basic model!** A crude, but identifiable skill emerges.
3 **Refinement of technique**. Very gradually errors are corrected and the quality of technique is improved.
4 **The 'fixing' of standard of performance**. The movement pattern becomes automatic and consistent.
5 **Physical adaptation**. Continued practising of a skill will bring about specific adaptation of all of the neuromuscular, anatomical and physiological systems involved.

Depending upon the amount of time devoted to skill development it can take many weeks, months and years to achieve the desired level of technical competence. The process from first to last is also affected by other factors such as:

- how complicated the action or sequence is
- the athlete's current level of technical ability
- if the athlete has learned any similar skills
- how quickly the athlete learns
- level of motivation
- current level of fitness
- the learning environment
- the ability of the coach.

The complexity of a technique can provide the learner with a challenge which you, the coach, will have to rise to. With a simple technique, such as a chest pass, the coach may wish to demonstrate and have the group copy his actions. This is known as the 'whole' method of teaching. But what happens if the action is more involved, as in pole vault? The coach may break the technique into smaller parts. Once each element is learned it can be tagged onto the previous one until the whole technique can be performed. This is known as the part–whole method of teaching. You could let the player have a try at the whole action first so that she or he has an idea of what is involved and then break it down. This is known as the whole–part–whole method, and there are other variations on a theme. How much a skill needs to be broken down will depend on the ability of the individual and your assessment of the situation.

And there's more! How do you organise the practices? Do you say, 'Working with a partner, everyone make 20 chest passes'? Or do you plan that they make ten, rest for a while and do ten more? This is called the distribution of practice. Is it better for a player to perform one large block of repetition of a skill, say 100 in one effort, or 10 at a time with a rest between? The coach has to make such decisions based on the ability of the player, the complexity of the skill and which is the best way for that individual.

By the repeated practice of a technique an accurate reproduction of perfect movement can be achieved. It is therefore essential that the correct technique is taught and learned from the outset. It is self-evident that if an incorrect action is ingrained all the efforts of athlete and coach have been wasted. You must be vigilant during any period of skill work that any inaccuracies are identified and corrected immediately.

In the development of a skill from first principles there is a process that all learners experience, usually referred to as the 'Learning Curve' (figure 12.5). It is characterised by a rapid improvement in technical accuracy that shifts to a very gradual rate of change.

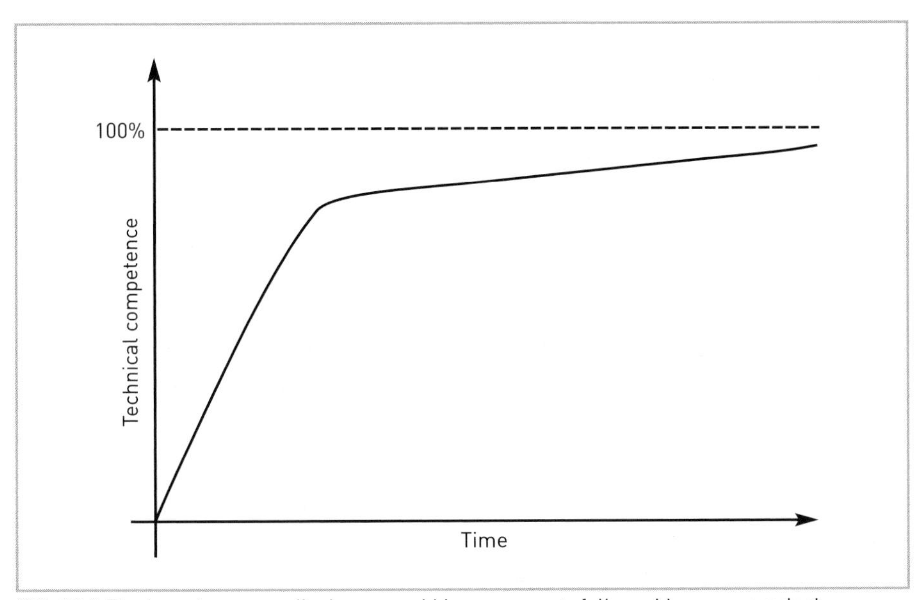

FIG. 12.5 The learning curve displays a rapid improvement, followed by more gradual refinement.

The slope of the graph follows the stages of skill learning very closely.

- The initial rapid rise occurs as quantity and effort produce crude technique.
- After a few sessions the athlete can produce movements of 50–60 per cent accuracy.
- As practice continues the rate of improvement slows and levels off at the 70–80 per cent level.
- The 80–100 per cent phase of skill learning is critical. It is during this period that continued practice will not only refine technique but ingrain the action into an automatic and consistent response. The difficulty arises in that after the rapid initial improvement changes now occur very slowly and often the athlete becomes despondent with no apparent progress. If the athlete and coach do not persevere during this period the establishment of excellent technique will not be achieved or stablised.

Just as there is 'learning curve' there is also a 'forgetting curve'! If skills are not practised on a regular basis they will deteriorate. The amount by which they decline is related to the degree of stability achieved. Research indicates that an ingrained and automatic skill will deteriorate relatively quickly over a two-year period to a 60 per cent level and very marginally after that. This seems to follow the old adage that you never forget how to ride a bike, no matter how long the gap may be and no matter how shaky the result! The research also supports the notion that, 'If you don't use it you lose it!' Lack of practise of a technique will also bring about a marked deterioration of those body systems that enable that movement to occur. This has major implications in injury prevention.

The Frequency of Training

The training environment for any sportsman or woman is characterised by work and more work! Techniques and sequences of movements are practised and refined through constant repetition. The specific conditioning that enables these skills to be more efficient and effective is achieved through commitment and application of consistent effort. It is also clear that every technique or action cannot be practised each session. Not only will the athlete become bored, but also doing so does not follow the Theory of Overcompensation requirement.

The length of a lesson and the frequency of breaks can be a major influence on the effectiveness of training, especially the learning process (see figure 12.6). Novice athletes should be restricted to an hour's training with a break after 25–30 minutes. Elite players can work for up to two hours with regular breaks for fluids.

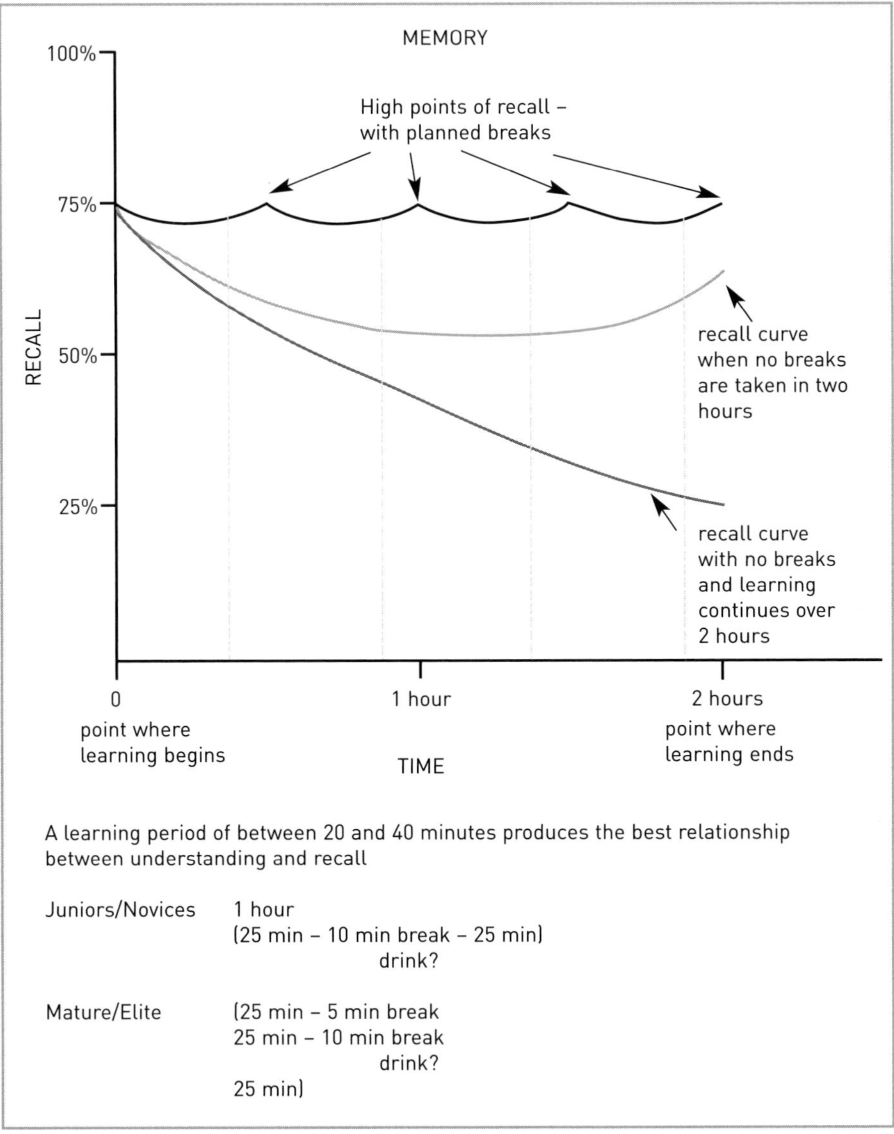

FIG. 12.6 The length of sessions and breaks can influence the rate of learning and performance retention.

When developing a technique, if it has been taught correctly, you will have related it to similar ones learned before. A previous skill is often the catalyst to a new one. Skills or sequences of movements can be grouped according to their similarities, such as types of pass or kicks. Any skill from the group that is practised in a session will have some beneficial effects on the others that are not included, even if only in preventing any 'forgetting'. This process is called the 'transfer of training'. Basically, an activity benefits from the practice of related skills and drills even though that exact one is not selected.

You must consider these aspects when planning sessions. Variety is the spice of life! Ring the changes in training on a regular basis. Since you cannot practise everything in one training unit ensure that in a given period of time all the drills and skills are covered specifically, and fully utilise the transfer of training theory to develop and maintain skill levels. Such variations will remove the predictability and boredom of unimaginative sessions and create a constant 'freshness' to the work.

The number of training units in a week will have a marked effect on the volume and content of work covered. Elite players may complete 20, 30 or more units of different work a week. Such a situation is ideal in terms of ensuring progress. Training less than this will reduce advancement.

References and Further Reading

Astrand, P-O. et al, *Textbook of Work Physiology* (4th edition), Human Kinetics, 2003

Benato, M. (ed.), *The Guinness Book of Football*, Guinness Publications, 1998

Cox, R. H., *Sport Psychology* (5th edition), McGraw-Hill, 2001

De Pauw, K. P. and Gavron, S. J., *Disability and Sport* (2nd edition), Human Kinetics, 1995

Dick, F. W., *Sports Training Principles* (4th edition), A & C Black, 2002

Edwards, P., Atkinson, J. and Gummerson, T., *Planning the Programme*, NCF, 1990

Gummerson, T., *Junior Martial Arts*, A & C Black, 1990

Gummerson, T., *Sports Coaching and Teaching*, A & C Black, 1992

Gummerson, T., *Teaching Martial Arts*, A & C Black, 1992

Jackson, S. A. and Csikszentmihali, M., *Flow in Sports*, Human Kinetics, 1999

Lee, M. J., *Coaching Children in Sport*, Spon Press, 1993

NCC, *Physical Education: The National Curriculum of England; Key Stage 1–4*

Paish, W. H., *Training for Peak Performance*, A & C Black, 1991

Selye, H., *The Stress of Life*, McGraw-Hill, 1978

Sport England, *Running Sport*, Sport England, 2002

Viru, A., *Adaptations in Sports Training*, CRC Press, 1994

Winnick, J. P. (ed.), *Adapted Physical Education and Sport* (4th edition), Human Kinetics, 1995

Youth Sport Trust, *The Young Athlete's Handbook*, YST, 2001

Index